the ORIGIN and EVOLUTION of the PRIESTHOOD

A Return to the Sources

alba house DIVISION OF THE SOCIETY OF ST. PAUL
STATEN ISLAND, N.Y. 10314

the ORIGIN and EVOLUTION of the PRIESTHOOD

James A. Mohler, S.J.

IMPRIMI POTEST:
   Walter L. Farrell, S.J.
   Provincial, Detroit Province

NIHIL OBSTAT:
   Donald A. Panella, S.T.L., S.S.L.
   Censor Librorum

IMPRIMATUR:
   Joseph P. O'Brien, S.T.D.
   Vicar General, New York
   October 21, 1969

The nihil obstat, imprimi potest and imprimatur are official declarations that
a book or pamphlet is free of doctrinal or moral error. No implication is
contained therein that those who have granted the nihil obstat, imprimi potest
or imprimatur agree with the contents, opinions or statements expressed.

Library of Congress Catalog Card Number: 73-110588

© 1970 by the Society of St. Paul, Staten Island, N.Y. 10314

SBN: 8189-0166-7

Designed, printed and bound in the U.S.A. by the Pauline Fathers and
Brothers of the Society of St. Paul at Staten Island, New York as a part of their
communications apostolate.

ACKNOWLEDGMENTS

Thomas Nelson and Sons, New York, for quotes from *The Apostolic Fathers,* R. Grant, ed.

Oxford University Press, New York, for quotes from the *Oxford Annotated Bible with the Apocrypha* and from R. Connolly's *Didascalia Apostolorum.*

Princeton University Press for quotes from *The Theodosian Code,* C. Pharr, tr.

Charles Scribner's Sons, New York, for quotes from the *Ante-Nicene Fathers,* A. Roberts and J. Donaldson, eds.

SPCK, London, for quotes from *A New Eusebius,* J. Stevenson, ed.

CONTENTS

PRINCIPAL ABBREVIATIONS

AC	*The Apostolic Constitutions* in Volume 7 of *The Ante-Nicene Fathers.*
AF	*The Apostolic Fathers,* R. Grant, ed., 6 vols., New York, Thomas Nelson and Sons, 1964-68
ANF	*The Ante-Nicene Fathers,* A. Roberts and J. Donaldson, eds., 10 vols., New York, Charles Scribner's Sons, 1926.
AT	*The Apostolic Tradition of Hippolytus,* tr., intro., and notes, B. Easton, Cambridge University Press, 1934.
CTh	*The Theodosian Code,* C. Pharr, tr., Princeton University Press, 1952.
DA	*Didascalia Apostolorum,* tr., intro., and notes, R. Connolly, Oxford at the Clarendon Press, 1929.
Hefele	*A History of the Church Councils,* C. Hefele, 5 vols., Edinburgh, T. & T. Clark, 1872.
NE	*A New Eusebius,* J. Stevenson, ed., London, SPCK, 1968.
NPNF	*A Select Library of The Nicene and Post-Nicene Fathers of the Christian Church,* P. Schaff, ed., New York, Charles Scribner's Sons, 1908-1914.

INTRODUCTION

Today's religions face a crisis in their ministries. The former prestige of the priest or minister as a community leader has diminished greatly except, perhaps, in mission areas. Even fifty years ago the local pastor with his seminary training was one of the best educated men in town. When most of the laity had at best a high school education, mothers saw in their children's vocation to the ministry a step up the social ladder into the professional class. The clergy were consulted on all sides from moral questions to problems in economics or politics.

But the educational level and social status of the Christian laity has been steadily rising with more and more attaining college degrees and professional status each year. Since seminary training has not always kept apace, in some parishes many of the laity are more highly educated than their clergy. Whereas in times past the pastor served as marriage counselor, psychologist, perhaps legal advisor, teacher, confessor and chief liturgical functionary, today many of these tasks have been taken over by professionally trained lay experts: psychiatrists, marriage counselors, social workers, and the like. Although the priest still reserves his liturgical presidency, even here the service has been opened to more and more lay participation.

Especially since Vatican II, lay Christians have taken over many tasks formerly reserved to the clergy so that the administration of schools, hospitals, social bureaus is now in the hands of competent laymen. Even on the missions, formerly the prerogative of religious orders and congregations, now lay missionaries, Peace Corps and Vista workers are taking active roles

in underdeveloped areas. Although increasing lay participation
in the ministries of the Church is an excellent development, it
may be contributing to the identity crisis of some of today's
clergy, especially older priests who have known the autocratic
monarchical prestige of former days.

As the gap narrows between laity and clergy, the question
is asked: what is the function of the priest today? Since many
of the laity are highly educated, the role of omnipotent and
omniscient pastor is no longer viable. Even his office of liturgical functionary has lessened, as has that of penitential judge
and counselor. Whatever the future may hold, we can never
return to the old monarchical pastor. The new ministry is one
of service.

A number of trends in the development of the ministry
have appeared since Vatican II. For example, many priests'
senates are now giving their support and counsel to their chief
presbyters, the bishops. The renewed diaconate is already helping to relieve the clergy shortage. The rise of the prophets has
caused much admiration and sometimes discomfort to the hierarchy as in days of old.

In this book we hope to take a close look at the origins
and evolution of the Christian presbyterate from its proto-type
in the Jewish sanhedrins through the New Testament and the
first four centuries. Because of the overlapping and interaction
of the early clerical functions, we must also examine the evolution of the episcopate, the diaconate and other developments.
By studying the problems of the early Christian ministry, we
may find surprising parallels to today's dilemmas. As in the
liturgy, centuries of accretions have sometimes obscured the
original significance of the first presbyters, which can only be
regained by a return to the sources.

As we shall see, the term *presbyteros* came over into Christianity from Judaism and was often used interchangeably with
episkopos. In the beginning in the Johannine school the presbyters gathered around their resident president, while in the

Pauline tradition the sanhedrins of elders were under the guidance of itinerant prophet-apostles. The presbyters were the elder brothers of the community, ruling, judging, giving good example. As the apostles began to settle down in the communities in the second century, they became monarchical guardians, chief admission officers, judges, teachers, and liturgical presidents of the local Christian communities.

As Christianity grew, of necessity the monarch was forced to delegate his powers first to chorbishops and then to presbyters to baptize, reconcile, and preside at the Eucharist. In the beginning delegation to presbyters was an emergency measure, but as the Church expanded, it became the norm. As the Church became more conscious of herself as the New Israel, the judging presbyters with their chief became the sons of Aaron under the high priest, the Eucharist became a sacrifice and levitical purity became the rule.

The relationship of the presbyters to their bishop, to the deacons and the laity, the custom of married clergy, the role of the prophet-teacher, the relationship of the monks to the city clergy, the identity crisis of the early presbyters especially in the Third and Fourth Centuries, all of these can be seen paralleled in the problems besieging today's ministers. This is why a study of the early ministry may prove fruitful to us today.

CHAPTER I

JEWISH PRESBYTERS

Councils of ruling elders may be found in most primitive societies and even in some advanced cultures such as the Hittites and Babylonians. It is natural for a community to respect the experienced wisdom of the elders sitting in council. These senates are common in third and second century B.C. in Egypt and Asia Minor. Undoubtedly the Jewish and Christian adaptation of ruling elders had its origins in contemporary practices in the Greco-Roman world.

A. Elders in the Old Testament

Frequent references to ruling presbyters or *zeqēnîm* may be found in the Old Testament. Sometimes they are called elders of Israel or of the city, people, Jerusalem, etc. The representatives of the people in political and religious matters, they are often associated with their leader when he exercises his authority as Moses did (Ex 3:18). At other times they are the governing body of the people as the elders of Gibeon (Jos 9:11) or of Gilead (Jgs 11:5ff). Frequently they act as judges (Dt 19:12; 21:3).

The establishment of a college of seventy elders by Moses (Nm 11:16-17) is of importance to us, for upon this body is based both the Jewish and the Christian concepts of the presbyterate. When Moses complained to the Lord that the burden of leading his people was too much for him, the Lord responded:

> Gather for me seventy men of the elders of Israel, whom you know to be the elders of the people and officers over them; and bring them to the tent of the meeting, and let them take their stand there with you. And I will come down and talk with you there, and I will take some of the spirit which is upon you and put it upon them, and they shall bear the burden of the people with you, that you may not bear it yourself alone. (Nm 11:16-17) [1]

So the Jewish elders of old with a share of Moses' spirit, help bear his burdens, yet remain subordinate to him.

During the monarchy when family, clan and tribe became of less importance, the elders diffused into cities and villages but it is possible that the body of ruling presbyters maintained itself by cooption. In the early monarchy, as the heads of tribes and clans, the elders formed the council of the king, and as the representatives of the people served as a check on his power.

---

1. Biblical quotes are from the Revised Standard Version as in the *Oxford Annotated Bible*.

B. *The Roman Period*

After the monarchy and the exile, elders were active in the time of Ezra (5:9) and in the period of the Maccabees (1 Mac 12:6). By the time of the Roman occupation every Jewish community in Palestine and in the diaspora had its own sanhedrin of *zeqēnîm*, elected by the people to administer the community affairs.[2] In the larger cities there was also an annually elected executive committee or prohedrin, chosen from among the elders. The local sanhedrins varied in numbers according to the size of the community, but the people always had a voice in their choice, even when the elders were appointed by the Nasi or his apostle. R. Isaac said, "One shall not appoint an elder over a community without first consulting that community" (Ber. 55a). Respecting heredity, they often chose the son of an elder.

Although not of the priestly line, the Jewish presbyters of the Roman era were, nevertheless, ordained with a laying on of hands [3] traced back to Moses' laying on of hands and sharing his spirit with Joshua, which Joshua, in turn, shared with the elders of Israel (Nm 27:18ff; Dt 34:9). This tradition passed to the prophets, then to the men of the Great Assembly from the time of Ezra to Simon the Righteous. Receiving the tra-

---

2. The Essene communities also had deliberative councils of elders including 12 laymen and 3 priests. Trained in the Law and community customs, they set high standards of holiness in charity, humility, faith and justice, irreproachable conduct and observance of the Law. At least in the beginning, the priests kept the authority in judicial and economic matters.

3. From the year 70 A.D. it seems that each scholar ordained his own disciples with a laying on of hands (*semikah*) (Yer. Sanh. 19a). After Hadrians' persecution during which ordination was forbidden, the Nasi alone ordained but by appointment (*minnuy*) rather than by a laying on of hands. Later the Nasi ordained with the approval of his Bet Din.

dition from Simon, Antigonus of Socho passed it on to the *zugoth* scholars (*Pirke Aboth* 1:1-4).

The local Jewish presbyterates of the Roman period were lay bodies dealing largely with civil government and judiciary matters. In the diaspora the presbyters served as a liaison between the Jewish community and the Gentile government. Sometimes they had the thankless task of collecting taxes for the Romans. Set apart by ordination and inspiration as the Judges of old, they interpreted the Law, the foundation of their decisions. Besides collecting and distributing alms to the needy, they had charge of the local synagogues and the temple in Jerusalem. Listed as officers of the synagogue, they were next in rank to the archisynagogues, with whom they are sometimes identified in early documents. They held the seats of honor which faced the people in the front of the synagogues (Tos. Meg. 3, 14).[4]

Let us now look at the Great Sanhedrin of elders in Jerusalem upon which the smaller local sanhedrins were modeled and depended. The Talmud [5] calls it the Great Sanhedrin (San-

---

4. In Matthew (23:1ff), Jesus criticizes some of the Pharisaic elders, as they no doubt criticized themselves, for seeking the chief seats. But they were to be heard since they had the privilege of occupying the Chair of Moses in the front of the synagogue. Their broad phylacteries and fringes, their choice seats and the honorific title of rabbi led some to ostentation. Jesus reproved their burdensome interpretations of the Law which they even laid on the proselytes in mission areas. Paul also reacted to this zeal among the Christian Pharisees. Finally the over-strict tithing and purifications of the Pharisees sometimes led to an externalism which could become hypocritical. See also C. Montefiore and H. Loewe in *A Rabbinic Anthology*, Cleveland, World Publishing Co., 1963, pp. 487-489.

5. How much can we know of the early sanhedrins by reading the tractate in the Mishnah, redacted in the third century? Does the Mishnah not reflect later developments at Jabneh or Tiberias? We must read the Mishnah with bifocals, perceiving contemporary traditions with the upper half, while striving to detect more ancient practices with the

hedrin Gedolah) which sits in the Hall of Hewn Stone adjacent to the temple. Including seventy members and the patriarch, its principal concern was religious law, the priests and the temple service.[6] A lesser sanhedrin of twenty-three acted as a supreme court in criminal cases as mentioned in the Gospels and Josephus. The great religious Sanhedrin, also called the Great Bet Din, as the highest religious authority, traced its origins back to Moses and the 70 elders (Sanh. 2a).[7] It was probably not established as such before the time of the second temple. First held under Ezra and Nehemiah as an occasional assembly, it was to become a permanent gerousia, consisting largely of priests and clan chiefs.

When Simeon the Righteous (c. 230 B.C.) called his Great Assembly (Keneset Ha-Gedolah), he admitted also plebian scholars. Whereas the government had formerly rested with the heads of families, elders, sheiks and priests, now it was to be shared with men of learning, often of humble origin. Aristocracy was evolving into sophocracy, a turning point in the history of Judaism. Antiochus III (c. 198 B.C.) extended tax exemptions to the whole gerousia, including not only the priests, but also the temple scribes and singers (Levites). Although John Hyrcanus (135-104 B.C.), siding with the aristocratic priests and clan chiefs, cast the scribes out of the Sanhedrin, they were to gain ascendancy again under Salome Alexandria (76-67 B.C.).

---

lower part. As with the gospels, it is sometimes difficult to separate the earlier from the later traditions.

6. A court of priests meeting in the chamber behind the Inner Shrine of the Temple at least at certain periods seems to have had the ultimate determination of the temple service, although they undoubtedly co-operated with the Sanhedrin. See L. Finkelstein, *The Pharisees*, Philadelphia, The Jewish Publication Society, 1966, pp. 726-731.

7. Finkelstein, *op. cit.*, pp. 576-577, 582-583, 607-608.

What qualifications were required of the elders of the Great Sanhedrin, the Great Bet Din? R. Jose B. Halafta says that they must be scholars, modest, popular with their fellow men, strong, courageous. They should have fulfilled three offices of gradually increasing dignity and responsibility, that is, a local judge and a member of two magistrates in Jerusalem (Tos. Hag. 2, 9; Sanh. 88b). R. Johanan (3C) said:

> None are to be appointed members of the sanhedrin, but men of stature, wisdom, good appearance, mature age, with a knowledge of sorcery, and who are conversant with all the seventy languages of mankind in order that the court should have no need of an interpreter (Sanh. 17a).[8]

Learning, knowledge of the scriptures, and fluency in languages are necessary even for members of the smaller sanhedrins.

The Great Bet Din sat in the Hall of Hewn Stone on the south side of the minor court of the temple where it supervised the temple service according to the Pharisaic tradition, appointed priests to officiate, supervised special rites, harvest tithes, arranged the calendar, provided copies of the Torah, interpreted the Law and guarded it against false teachers. In New Testament times the leadership of the Sanhedrin may have alternated between the Pharisees and the Sadducees. Although the New Testament often describes the high priest as the head of the Sanhedrin (Mk 14:60; Jn 18:24; Acts 5:21),[9] in Acts (5:34, 40) the Pharisee Gamaliel shows true leadership. In the New Testament writings the Sanhedrin sometimes consists of chief priests and scribes (Lk 22:66); rulers (some of

---

8. *The Babylonian Talmud, Seder Nezikin, Sanhedrin I,* I. Epstein, tr., London, The Soncino Press, 1935, p. 87.

9. See also Josephus (*Ant* 14, 8, 5; 4, 8, 14).

whom were priests), elders and scribes (Acts 4:5-6); high priests and elders (Acts 4:23; 5:21). The executive committee, prohedrin, met in a chamber by the side of the Hall of Hewn Stone. Chosen annually, it included ten members plus the high priest and the temple treasurer. When in session, the elders of the Sanhedrin sat in a semicircle around the Nasi with two or three scribes and three rows of scholars in front. It was usual for new elders to be chosen from these scholars (Sanh. 36b, 37a).

Josephus, upon orders from the Jerusalem Sanhedrin set up courts of elders to help him rule Galilee in the war against the Romans. He knew that a sharing of power with the local sanhedrins was essential for the cooperation of the people. He chose 70 elders as a great sanhedrin to rule all of Galilee, and seven judges in each city to hear lesser cases. Capital crimes were to be heard by Josephus and the 70 (*War* 2, 20, 5). He accused the zealots and Idumaeans of setting up dishonest sanhedrins of elders (*War* 4, 5, 4).

After the year 70 A.D., the Jerusalem Sanhedrin continued as the rabbinical academy at Jabneh under the patriarchs of the family of Hillel, then at Tiberias until the fourth century. Upon election to membership, the councilors were ordained by the laying on of hands (until 135) of the patriarch with two of his elders. From the time of Jabneh local Jewish courts of elders consisted largely of rabbis so that in the Talmud sometimes rabbis and elders seem interchangeable. By his ordination, the elder receives a degree, the title of rabbi, and the authority to judge cases of *kenas* (Sanh. 13b). One of the Hebrew words for office is *rabbanut*. Before appointment to office the scholar (*haber*) is carefree, but once he receives the robe (*tallit*) of office, he bears the burden of the community (Exod. R. Yitro, 27, 9, on 18, 1).

Important members of the Sanhedrin were the apostles

(*selîhîm*),[10] who as the foremost ordained scholars of their generation were empowered to act in place of the Nasi. Epiphanius (*Heresies* 1, 2, 30, 4), said that the apostles of his time (4 c.) ranked after the patriarch. Sitting next to him, these scholars counseled him in matters concerning the Law. As the Nasi's apostles, they carried the message of Jewish piety and learning to the diverse Jewish communities, and in turn, informed the Nasi of the situation in the diaspora. Acting as fund-raisers and administrators, they were also delegated to proclaim new moons and festivals, traveling as far as a 13 day journey from the Bet Din. Carrying letters from the Nasi, announcing their mission and introducing them as apostles, they presided over local courts and even had the authority to appoint ruling presbyters when requested by the community.[11]

Epiphanius (*Heresies* 1, 2, 30, 11) tells of a fourth century apostle of the Nasi who ruled the Jewish communities of Cilicia, traveling around the country with the authority to remove archisynagogues, priests, elders, and precentors. It seems that the Nasi also appointed resident apostles as at Antioch where they ruled for a term of one year. The ordination of scholars by the Nasi at Gaza, Rome and Damascus suggests that they may have been apostles with the authority to rule in place of the Nasi. They are called "primates" or "little patriarchs" in Roman documents such as the Code of Theodosius (16, 8, 8) and the Code of Justinian (1, 9, 7).[12]

---

10. Although the *apostoloi* of the Talmud were probably a development of the Jabneh Sanhedrin, the Jerusalem Sanhedrin may have had similar delegates. Besides being a delegate of the court (*Sheliah Bet Din*) the Jewish apostle could be a delegate of the community (*Sheliah Zibbur* [*apostolos ekklēsias?*]), representing the community in prayer or good works. They travelled in pairs, living frugally as Paul and Barnabas did.

11. H. Mantel, *Studies in the History of the Sanhedrin*, Cambridge, Mass., Harvard University Press, 1961, pp. 190-198.

12. *Ibid.*, 204, 205.

From Moses and the 70 the tradition of ruling and judging elders came down to the first Christian century. The local sanhedrins probably dependent on their apostle and ultimately on the Nasi in Jerusalem were likely models for the first Christian presbyterates. Many of their functions were similar, namely, ruling, judging, forming a liaison with the civil government. From this basic structure under the guidance of the Spirit was to develop the Christian ministry.

CHAPTER II

CHRISTIAN PRESBYTERS OF THE NEW TESTAMENT

The Christian ministry of the New Testament has affinities with the Jewish structures of the first century including the synagogue, ruling elders, itinerant apostles, the Nasi, and a central Sanhedrin. Some would say that it was difficult for the Romans to distinguish Christians from Jews in this period. Until the parting of the ways Christian Jews attended the synagogue regularly, observed the Torah, and, in general, kept the Jewish customs. As Christianity moved to the Gentiles of the West, and Jerusalem the center of Christian Judaism was destroyed, Christian Judaism gradually died out, but not without leaving a permanent impact on the nascent Church and her ministry.

In the gospels the Christian ministry is first discipleship to the rabbi Jesus of Nazareth and then apostleship with the delegated authority of the master. Sending his disciples to proclaim his message, Jesus gave them the power over unclean spirits, the power to heal and preach the gospel. He also gave them travel instructions. Without money or provisions, they should live off the hospitality of those who believe. And those who do not receive them should be cast off. The gospel will bring persecution and will even divide families against each other. As the itinerant missionaries of the infant Church, the apostles should proclaim the Messiah by their lives, making disciples of the nations (Mt 28:18-20), baptizing and teaching all that Jesus had commanded. The Twelve are the apostles par excellence under the leadership of Peter their spokesman in faith and love.

A. Paul

Although Paul may have been an apostle of the Sanhedrin (Acts 9:1-2; 26:10-12), before his conversion, now he proudly serves his new Nasi, Jesus Christ. When challenged by the Corinthians, he stoutly defended his new apostleship. Did he have a letter of recommendation as the other apostles had? "You yourselves are our letter of recommendation, written on your hearts, to be known and read by all men; and you show that you are a letter from Christ delivered by us, written not with ink, but with the Spirit of the living God, not on tablets of stone, but on tablets of human hearts" (2 Cor 3:2-3). As an apostle Paul brings gifts (1 Cor 1:7), preaches Jesus Christ crucified (1:23), building the firm foundation of the Church (3:10-11). Paul is the servant of Christ and the steward of God (4:1), proclaiming the gospel and serving all.

Having seen the risen Christ, Paul was personally commissioned by him as an apostle to preach the gospel (Gal 1:11-16; 1 Cor 15:8-10). Although in Acts (13:2-3) we find Paul sent off as a missionary by the church of Antioch (*apostolos ekklēsias;* c.f. 2 Cor 8:23), he always maintained that his apostleship was directly from Jesus Christ (*apostolos Christou;* c.f. 2 Cor 11:13). As a Christian apostle, Paul assumes many tasks similar to those of the Jewish apostles of the Sanhedrin, for example: he judges (1 Cor 5:1-13), reconciles (2 Cor 1: 23-2:11), punishes, admonishes not to take differences to the civil courts (1 Cor 6:1-8), settles marriage problems (1 Cor 7), admonishes not to eat meat offered to idols (1 Cor 7), cautions about abuses during the meal accompanying the Eucharist (1 Cor 11:17-33), raises funds (1 Cor 16:1-4; 2 Cor 8-9).

Paul's primary apostolic duty is to proclaim the gospel, sharing in the passion of Jesus Christ. Once the mission is established he acts as judge, counselor, teacher, liturgical president, reconciler, but always as the servant of the community. Paul often refers to his work for the Church as his ministry (*diakonia*). He is a minister of Jesus Christ, of God, and of the gospel (2 Cor 3:6; 11:23; Col 1:7, 25; 4:7).

In describing the ministry, Paul's terminology is sometimes ambiguous intermingling offices and charisms. For example, in Romans he speaks of the charisms of prophecy, service, of the teacher, exhorter, almoner, advocate, and almsgiver (12:6-8). While he lists church offices in First Corinthians (12:28) as: apostles, prophets, teachers, wonder workers, healers, helpers, administrators, and speakers in tongues, in Ephesians (4:11) (probably not Paul's) are listed: apostles, prophets, evangelists, shepherds, and teachers. Whereas Ephesians seems to give a list of officers, the First Corinthians' list mixes offices such as apostles, prophets, and administrators with functions such as healers and speakers in tongues. Nevertheless, both offices and functions are charisms.[1]

In Philippians (1:1) Paul writes to the saints of Philippi with their guardians (*episkopoi*) and ministers (*diakonoi*). Also he mentions his fellow workers such as Epaphroditus and

---

1. See J. McKenzie, *Authority in the Church*, N.Y. Sheed and Ward, 1966, p. 70.

Clement (2:25; 4:3). In his discussions of the various types
of ministry, Paul usually gives precedence to the charismatic
apostle-prophet-teachers to whom he belonged, but he would
also consider administration as a gift, albeit of a lower order.
Paul was a prophet-teacher in Antioch (Acts 13:1-3). This
is proper, for the Jewish religious teachers considered themselves the successors of the prophets. Jesus himself fits into
this tradition. In First Corinthians (12:28) Paul ranks teachers
next in line to the prophets and second after the apostles. Later
(14:1ff) he describes a prophet as one who teaches men for
the encouragement, consolation and edification of the Church.
So prophecy and teaching overlapped with each other and
with apostleship. In Ephesians (2:20; 3:5) the prophets are
ranked next to the apostles as in Corinthians (1 Cor 12:28).
The itinerant prophet-apostles are mentioned later in Didache
(11:3ff).

In his First Letter to the Corinthians Paul urges them to
be subject to those early converts of the house of Stephanas,
who seem to be the elders of the community (16:15-16). They
have devoted their lives to the ministry of the saints, making
their home a center of hospitality, service, and liturgy, a very
early house-church. Some would see in the helpers and administrators of Corinth (1 Cor 12:28) counterparts of the
deacons and guardians of Philippi (Phil 1:1) and the helpers
and advocates of Rome (Rom 12:6-8). Of all the ministries
at the time of Paul, the first to receive an official status as
officers of the community are the guardians and deacons. As
the least charismatic and least peripatetic of the ministers, they
could more easily assume the day to day direction of the
Church. Paul does not mention presbyters as such, but they
may have been included under the guardians.

B. *Acts of the Apostles*

In the first twelve chapters of Acts the Twelve apostles
assume the leadership in the Jerusalem church. They select

Matthias, one who had been with them from the baptism of John and had witnessed the resurrection, to take the place of Judas (1:22). As their Jewish counterparts, the Christian apostles are officers of the first rank. They proclaim the gospel and defend their rights before the Sanhedrin (4:5-21; 5:22-42). To free themselves for missionary work, they appointed seven helpers (6:1-6). Although the Seven are traditionally regarded as deacons, their functions are more like those of the presbyters or episcopals (20:17-28). The apostles received and distributed the goods which members of the Christian community had donated to the common cause (4:32-35). They judged the erring (5:1-11), sent Peter and John as missionaries to Samaria (8:14) and Barnabas to Antioch (11:22). Alms are brought to Jerusalem by Paul and Barnabas to be distributed to the needy (11:29-30).

In the first twelve chapters of Acts Peter is the leader of the Jerusalem church. He is their spokesman at meetings, proclaims the gospel, defends the Church before the Sanhedrin, suggests filling the empty place of Judas, acts for the Twelve in the collecting of goods, evangelizes Gentiles and defends his action before all. Although little is said of Peter after chapter twelve, he may have been engaged in missionary work among the diaspora Jews (Gal 2:7-8), while James, the brother of the Lord, took over the Jerusalem church and Paul the missions to the Gentiles. Even in the first part of Acts Peter's leadership is not absolute for he rules in conjunction with the other apostles and the Church. In fact, his baptism of the Gentiles is challenged (11:1-18), and Paul rebukes him for his fear of the circumcision party from Jerusalem (Gal 2:11-14). In this instance and at the council of Jerusalem Peter seems to show deference to James.

In Acts we find evidence at Jerusalem of a Christian sanhedrin composed of apostles and presbyters. Far from being merely temporal administrators, the Jerusalem Christian presbyters partook of the Apostles' authority in doctrinal decisions as at the Council of Jerusalem, where final judgment was made concerning the circumcision of Gentile converts.[2] It is notable that the apostles and presbyters not only discuss the problem together, but share in the ultimate decision as first spoken by James, the Lord's brother and president of the Jerusalem Christian sanhedrin, the decision-making body of the infant Church, the interpreter of the Law and the guardian of tradition.

> The brethren, both the apostles and the elders to the brethren who are of the Gentiles in Antioch, Syria and Cilicia, greetings . . . . It has seemed good to the Holy Spirit and to us to lay upon you no greater burden than these necessary things: that you abstain from what has been sacrificed to idols and from blood and from what is strangled and from unchastity. If you keep yourselves from these, you will do well. Farewell. (15:23, 28-29)

Although not required to observe the law of circumcision, the Gentile converts should keep the Noachian precepts. Upon this encyclical letter Paul and Barnabas are to base their preaching to the Gentiles (16:4).

Although the apostles and presbyters are mentioned together at Jerusalem, the apostles are always mentioned first, for they are of higher rank and so precede the elders, but share with them doctrinal and disciplinary decisions.

In Jerusalem the Christian Jewish presbyters, as good Jewish laymen, frequented the temple and the synagogue where they read the Torah and prayed. They partook of the Eucharist,

---

2. The necessity of the circumcision of proselytes, debated among the rabbis of the time, was favored more by the Palestinian rabbis than by those of the diaspora. See *The Jewish Encyclopedia*, vol. 4, K. Kohler, "Circumcision," pp. 94-96; I. Abrahams, *Studies in Pharisaism and the Gospels*, N.Y., KTAV, 1967, vol. 1, p. 37f.

perhaps in the home of James. Following rabbinical tradition and especially the example of their Master, they visited the sick, praying over them and anointing them in a sacral manner (Jas 5:14-15). Sometimes we find the Jerusalem presbyterate acting independently of the apostles as when they advised Paul to purify himself in order to allay the suspicions of certain Jewish Christians zealous for the Law (21:17-26). Many of those who pushed for a stricter observance of the Law were Christian Pharisees (15:5).

Perhaps it would be good at this point to say something of James, the brother of the Lord, the president of the Jerusalem Christian sanhedrin. We have already seen his presidency at the Council of Jerusalem. Paul respected his office and was careful to report to him and the college after his third missionary journey (21:18). Peter, too, respected James and his representatives (Gal 2:11-14). Since James is never clearly called one of the Twelve, scholars are hesitant to identify him with James of Alpheus. As leader of the Jerusalem Christians, in place of his brother Jesus, he has the full power to preach, teach, judge, interpret the Law, and preside. Rather than an itinerant missionary as Peter and Paul, James remains in residence at Jerusalem, a prototype of the monarchical bishops of succeeding generations, centers of unity, orthodoxy, guardians of tradition, instruments of the Holy Spirit.

As a blood relative of Jesus, brother of Joses, Simon and Jude of Nazareth, James was honored by the early Christians as a living remembrance of the Lord. He, in turn, Eusebius (*History of the Church* 4, 22, 4) tells us, was succeeded in the exiled Christian community of Pella by Symeon, son of Clopas, an uncle of Jesus. As Colson remarks,[3] the Jews had a strong

---

3. J. Colson, *L'évêque dans les communautes primitives,* Unam Sanctam, N. 21, Paris, Cerf, 1951, p. 25.

tradition of honoring the surviving relatives of fallen heroes. Witness the Maccabean succession.

Under James the Jerusalem Church was, indeed, the mother church of primitive Christianity, sending missionaries, judging disputes, and guarding tradition. Surrounding James, the Lord's brother in lieu of the Lord, himself, the Jerusalem Christian sanhedrin represents the complete *ekklēsia,* to which the mission churches look for initiative, leadership and approval, yet by no means diminishing the importance of the Twelve, who were Jesus' personal choice to carry his message to the world. It is interesting to note that little is said of the Twelve outside of the Gospels and little is mentioned of Peter in the second part of Acts. Josephus tells us (*Antiquities* 20, 9, 1) that James was held in high regard by all. The Ebionite literature may be exaggerating when it claims that James sent Peter to Caesarea to meet Simon Magus, and that no one coming from Jerusalem may teach without a written letter from James, who is the "Bishop of bishops." [4]

The Antioch mission of the Jerusalem church gives us important clues concerning the organization of the early Christian community. When Palestinian Christian Jews, scattered by persecution, preached the gospel in Antioch, many Greeks believed. Upon hearing the news of large conversions in Antioch, the Jerusalem church sent Barnabas as an apostle (11:20-22) to organize the Christian community there. Together with Saul, Barnabas will form the *ekklēsia* there which was the first to be called Christian. Thus develop two forms of organization in the infant Church: at Jerusalem the Church is governed by a sanhedrin of presbyters under the presidency of James, while in Antioch the Christian community is under a delegated apostle, living temporarily in the community in order to organize it. In

---

4. *The Recognitions of Clement,* L. 1, ch. 72; L. 4, ch. 35; *The Epistle of Clement to James,* init.

Jewish tradition the Nasi's power to appoint an apostle to rule over the Antioch community seems to date from an early period, perhaps paralleling that of early Christianity,[5] although the Nasi had more power over the diaspora after 135.

In the Antioch community a nucleus of prophet-teachers including Saul grouped around Barnabas. With their model as Jesus Christ, they studied Torah and strove to explain Jesus and his kingdom in a biblical manner. Teaching was an important charism in the early Church, often overlapping with apostleship and prophecy. False teachers were common and early documents are constantly warning against them.

The prophet-teachers of Antioch form a sort of itinerant hierarchy from which were chosen Saul and Barnabas to be sent off with a laying on of hands to do missionary work elsewhere (13:2-3). The Antioch mission was to remain dependent on its apostles and ultimately on the mother church of Jerusalem. As Paul and Barnabas traveled throughout the diaspora, they appointed presbyters to govern the local churches (14:23), but probably not without consulting the local community. These local presbyterates leaned upon their founding apostles for instruction and leadership, as the local Jewish communities in the area may have depended on their traveling apostle.[6]

On his last journey Paul called together his presbyter-guardians from Ephesus to Miletus where he cautioned them of the dangers of the future. All were saddened that they would never see their apostle again.

Take heed to yourselves and to all the flock, in which the Holy Spirit has made you guardians, to feed the church of the Lord, which he obtained with his own blood. I know that after my departure fierce wolves will come in among

---

5. Mantel, *op. cit.*, pp. 203-204.
6. Mantel, *op. cit.*, p. 206.

you, not sparing the flock; and from among your own selves will arise men speaking perverse things, to draw away the disciples after them. Therefore, be alert, remembering that for three years I did not cease night or day to admonish every one with tears. And now I commend you to God and to the word of his grace, which is able to build you up and to give you the inheritance among all those who are sanctified. (20:28-32)

Dispensing the truth, watching over digressions, they must guard the unity of tradition against the false teachers. As elder brothers of the Christian community, they must feed, guide, give good example to the younger members. In this context the presbyters (20:17) and guardians (20:28) are synonymous with the latter describing the principal function of the former. It seems that guardian (*episkopos*) was a common title for officers of Greek communities of the time. Later the title will be used properly of the president of the presbyterate. Here it is too early to claim such a distinction. The Ephesian sanhedrin probably had the same function as the Jerusalem one, namely, governing, guiding, judging, teaching, admitting new members, collecting and dispensing alms, partaking in the synagogue liturgy, the Eucharist, visiting and anointing the sick, but with the basic difference of a dependence upon an itinerant apostle, rather than a resident president as James of Jerusalem.

C. Pastoral Epistles

It is in the Pastoral Epistles to Timothy and Titus that the function of the Christian presbyters develops and a distinction begins to appear between the college of presbyters and its guardian president. Yet although the Pastorals reflect a more highly developed Church structure, they are evidently before Clement (c. 95).

Frequently the question is asked: are the terms *presbyteros* and *episkopos* interchangeable in the Pastoral Letters, or is *episkopos* reserved only for the president of the sanhedrin of presbyters? Although the terminology is far from stratified, an order of precedence can be detected for *episkopoi* are always mentioned before *diakonoi* as in Philippians (1:1). Paul and his colleagues had established presbyters at Ephesus and Crete as guardians of the Christian communities there (Acts 20:28; Tit 1:5ff). Spicq [7] notes that the guardians (*episkopoi*) are never mentioned among the apostles, prophets, or teachers, that is, among the missionaries of the Church. It seems that they are rather the leaders of the established Christian community.

The guardian (*episkopos*) presides over the Christian community (1 Tim 3:4-5), guiding the family of God as a father. He is the administrator (*oikonomos*) of the *ekklēsia,* the pastor of the flock and cultic officer of the Christian assembly. As the official representative of the Church (1 Tim 3:1ff) and head of the Christian family, he receives traveling Christians hospitably, has charge of the collection and distribution of alms. Moreover, he must be knowledgeable in doctrine, for teaching and guarding tradition are his major responsibilities (Tit 1:9).

Were the episcopals and the presbyters the same people? Certainly their proper virtues are described analogously in the Pastoral Epistles (1 Tim 3:1ff; Tit 1:5ff), especially in the letter to Titus (1:7), where *episkopos* is substituted for *presbyteroi* as if the terms were interchangeable. Elsewhere when *episkopoi* are mentioned, *presbyteroi* are not (Phil 1:1). And when Timothy is advised of the respect due to presbyters, episcopals are not mentioned. But the essential function of presbyters as guardians is to preside (1 Tim 5:17). In Ephesus all

---

7. C. Spicq, *St. Paul, les épîtres pastorales,* Paris, LeCoffre, 1947, p. 87.

the elders seem to be called guardians (Acts 20:17, 28). Spicq [8] maintains that the terms: presbyters, leaders (*hēgoumenoi*), presidents, pastors, and guardians are interchangeable in the Pastoral Epistles and concern the same office of government in the local churches. However, with the exception of the late letters (e.g., 2 & 3 Jn) *presbyteroi* are always in the plural while *episkopos* usually is in the singular with the definite article (e.g., 1 Peter 2:25).

The presbyters seem to have been in the Church from the beginning but the guardians appear for the first time at Ephesus in the year 58 (Acts 20:28) and at Philippi in 60-62 (Phil 1: 1). Although the custom of ruling presbyters came over from Judaism, there is no direct Jewish counterpart to the guardians, despite attempts to link them with the Essene *mevaqqer* [9] and the archisynagogue of contemporary Judaism. Some Greek officials, however, were known as *episkopoi*. We might conclude with Spicq [10] that although presbyters and guardians are often employed one for the other, they do not mean absolutely the same thing. Thus there probably was a progressive evolution in the hierarchy of the early Church. From the beginning were apostles and presbyters, to whom were joined deacons. Whereas the elders teach, guide and govern, the deacons assume the more humble tasks. Presbyters are called guardians to underline their administrative, presidential and pastoral office (e.g., Acts 20:28). At this point in Acts *episkopos* is a common name and not a title of dignity, for all the presbyters have the duty of presiding, feeding, and watching over the flock.

---

8. *St. Paul, les épîtres pastorales*, p. 91.

9. The *mevaqqer* (visitor or controller) bore some resemblance to the guardian. Along with a priest he ruled the Essene communities. Generally, a layman 30-50 years old, he was knowledgeable in Law and language, admitted and instructed neophytes, shepherded his flock and was the disciplinary and financial officer.

10. *St. Paul, les épîtres pastorales*, p. 92.

Yet in the Pastoral Epistles *episkopos* seems to be distinguished from the court of elders as a definite office (*episkopē*) in the Church, although it has not yet reached the monarchical episcopacy of the second century, for there is not one reference to the position of the guardian vis-à-vis the other presbyters. It would seem, however, that at this stage all the elders were not guardians in the evolved sense of the word. Thus the episcopacy which was common to all the elders at Ephesus in 58 and at Philippi 5 years later is henceforth reserved to a specially qualified person, who, nevertheless, still considers himself a presbyter. So a descriptive term applied to all the presbyters becomes a technical one reserved to their head, who is the one steward and father of the Christian community. The episcopal performs a good work (1 Tim 3:1). As God's steward he oversees the evangelization. He is the presiding elder, father, guardian, judge, teacher, administrator, exemplar and cultic president.

An elder-guardian must have the highest qualifications in order to lead the Church in a manner worthy of his office. First Timothy (3:1-7) is specific in its requirements for the episcopal chair.

The saying is sure: if any one aspires to the office of bishop, he desires a noble task. Now a bishop must be above reproach, the husband of one wife, temperate, sensible, dignified, hospitable, an apt teacher, no drunkard, not violent, but gentle, not quarrelsome, and no lover of money. He must manage his household well, keeping his children submissive and respectful in every way; for if a man does not know how to manage his own household, how can he care for God's Church? He must not be a recent convert, or he may be puffed up with conceit and fall into the condemnation of the devil. Moreover, he must be well thought of by outsiders, or he may fall into reproach and the snare of the devil.

The directions to Titus are equally strong (1:5-9):

> This is why I left you in Crete, that you might amend what
> was defective and appoint elders in every town as I directed
> you, if a man is blameless, the husband of one wife, and his
> children are believers and not open to the charge of being
> profligate and insubordinate. For a bishop, as God's steward
> must be blameless; he must not be arrogant or quick-tem-
> pered or a drunkard or violent or greedy for gain, but
> hospitable, a lover of goodness, master of himself, upright,
> holy, and self-controlled. He must hold firm to the sure
> word as taught so that he may be able to give instruction
> in sound doctrine and also to confute those who contradict
> it.

Although the two lists are not exact copies, they are analogous.

Two virtues are most notable and include lesser ones. First,
the Christian leader must be irreproachable in his morals. Secondly, he must show qualities of government illustrated by a
good father of a family. As the official representative of the
Church, he must be above all reproach even from outsiders.
He must be in control of his passions, temperate, chaste, sober.
A devoted husband, he is a wise and prudent father to his
family, exercising firm, but gentle authority over his children
and his whole household, welcoming strangers to his hospitality
as he would Christ. He must be sensible, dignified, proper, self-
controlled, humble, not covetous, and not using his office as
a way to personal power and fame. He should be kind, merciful, peaceful, a wise and learned teacher and steward of tradition, guarding it from the attacks of false teachers.

There are remarkable parallels between the Lukan parables
of Stewardship (Lk 12:42-48; 16:1-14) and the Pauline direc-
tives to Timothy and Titus. In Luke the steward (*oikonomos*)
who is given charge of the master's house and servants in his

absence, must render an account of his stewardship when the master returns. The unfaithful steward, taking advantage of his master's absence, acted in an arrogant manner, so the faithful and prudent steward is placed by the master over all his goods (Lk 12:44). Those who are faithful in small things will be faithful in greater (Lk 16:1-13). The most important role of the guardian in the Pastorals is his fidelity to his master. His charge is the sacred treasure of the kingdom of heaven placed under his stewardship as a trust. In general, the virtues of the elder-guardian in the Pastorals parallel those of the prudent and faithful steward in Luke, showing a Lukan influence.[11]

It is interesting to note that although there may be Lukan nuances in the lists of virtues required of the early Church leaders, these could well be demanded of any contemporary leader civil or religious. As Spicq says,[12] we cannot presuppose that the first ministers of the Church were great heroes of virtue, nor can we assume that those who have a charism of government are by that very fact more elevated by grace. This would presuppose a grading of morality according to office and would overlook the universality of the call to evangelical perfection, applying equally to all Christians. This is reflected in the virtues required of the elderly (Tit 2:1-5). The presbyterian virtues outlined in the Pastorals may be found also in Stoic, Greek and Roman contemporary documents which listed the qualifications for political, military or religious office. So the Pastorals demand of Christian leaders a basic morality quite acceptable even according to pagan standards. Although the Pastoral lists may well have been adapted from contemporary customs, they do have a Lukan flavor so that the life of a Christian steward, presbyter or guardian, and the lives of his

---

11. See C. Spicq, "L'origine évangélique des vertus episcopales selon S. Paul," *Revue Biblique,* January, 1946, pp. 36-46.

12. *St. Paul, les épîtres pastorales,* p. 238.

whole family must be above reproach, a living image of the absent Master.

In the first letter to Timothy (5:17-25) we find outlined several problems that had arisen concerning the Ephesian presbyters.

> Let the elders who rule well be considered worthy of a double honor, especially those who labor in preaching and teaching. For the Scripture says, "You shall not muzzle an ox when it is treading out the grain," and "The laborer deserves his wages." (5:17-18)

Since the elders are spending so much of their time in preaching and teaching, the faithful should help support them. Although Jewish priests lived off the altar, the elders and rabbis were generally self-supporting, but in many ways privileged. Paul worked as a tent-maker, although as an apostle, he had a right to sustenance from the Church (1 Cor 9). Evidently the Christians of Ephesus had complained about having to support their elders, as those in Corinth had protested earlier.

The presbyterate itself is worthy of honor, and if exercised well, even more so, and especially those presbyters who are engaged in the exhausting and time consuming work of preaching and teaching. But the false teachers who use their ministry for personal gain are not to be supported (1 Tim 6:5f; Tit 1:11).

The correction of erring presbyters was another problem at Ephesus. "Never admit any charge against an elder except on the evidence of two or three witnesses. As for those who persist in sin, rebuke them in the presence of all, so that the rest may stand in fear" (1 Tim 5:19-20).

Although Jewish legal tradition was quite protective of the rights of the accused, in cases involving presbyters even greater care should be taken because of their greater dignity. Christian leaders should be above suspicion, but they are human and so erring, and some may have been falsely accused. No accusation is to be accepted against an elder unless on the testimony of two or three witnesses. But if it is firmly established that an elder has sinned, he is to be rebuked in front of all to serve as a warning to the rest. A final admonition concerns ordination by the laying on of hands, a custom derived from the Jewish ordination of elders and rabbis.

> Do not be hasty in the laying on of hands, nor participate in another man's sins; keep yourself pure .... The sins of some men are conspicuous, pointing to judgment, but the sins of others appear later. So also good deeds are conspicuous; and even when they are not, they cannot be hidden. (5:22, 24-25)

Following directly on the counsels for correction, Timothy is reminded that the basic root of faltering elders is a too hasty laying on of hands, that is, ordaining unsuitable men to fill the rapidly increasing demands for leaders in the Church. Above all, the ordinand should display the virtues previously outlined (3:1-7), for he who ordains one who is unproven is responsible for the sins and scandals that he preaches. Since it is difficult to judge the worthy, extreme caution should be had.

D. *The Shepherd-Guardians of 1 Peter*

The author exhorts his fellow presbyters of Pontus, Galatia, Cappadocia, Asia, and Bithynia:

> Tend the flock of God that is your charge, supervising (*episkopōuntes*), not by constraint but willingly, not for shameful gain but eagerly, not as domineering over those in your charge but being examples to the flock. And when the chief Shepherd is manifested, you will obtain the un-

fading crown of glory. Likewise you that are younger be subject to the elders. Clothe yourselves, all of you, with humility toward one another, for "God opposes the proud, but gives grace to the humble." (1 Pet 5:2-5)

Here presbyters, episcopals and pastors seem to be the same. They should be models of Jesus Christ, their chief Shepherd. Serving their office freely and not for shameful gain as the false teachers do, they should not seek to dominate, lording it over their flocks, but rather offer good example to them. Every presbyter, then, takes the place of Christ as pastor and guardian of souls. Thus the elder-guardian-pastors participate in the one pastorate of Jesus Christ, for this reason the faithful should be obedient to them. It would seem that as at Ephesus, Crete and Corinth, the elders of the Asian communities form acephalous colleges in which the pastorship or guardianship is assumed by many and not by one, remaining dependent on an itinerant apostle for instruction and guidance.

E. The Johannine Tradition

The use of the title of elder by the author of the Second and Third Letters of John seems to parallel that of the First Letter of Peter (5:1), namely, a witness to the sufferings and a partaker in the glory of Jesus Christ. The Johannine tradition seems to parallel that of Jerusalem where the college of elders was grouped around its resident president, James. This was the pattern to be followed by Ignatius, Polycarp, Irenaeus, etc. Colson [13] interprets the angels of the seven churches of the Book of Revelation (2 & 3) as local church presidents in whom John sees the incarnation of Church unity as guardians and conservers of the faith.

---

13. *L'évêque dans les communautes primitives,* Unam Sanctam, N. 21, Paris, Cerf, 1951, p. 81.

G. Dix [14] sees the heavenly throne and the 24 elders of Revelation (4:2-4) reflecting the early Christian liturgy, perhaps at Ephesus where the president sat on his throne covered with white cloth. He faces the people across the eucharistic table with the 24 elders forming a semi-circle around him and the deacons stationed on either side of the throne. The description reminds one of the local Jewish Sanhedrin at Ephesus which probably had 23 elders seated in a semicircle, perhaps with an apostle presiding and two or three scribes in attendance. Ignatius describes a parallel liturgy in Antioch in 115 (Magn. 6:1). The semicircle of elders around the bishop facing the people with the helping deacons seems to have been a rather normal form of early Christian worship.

Colson [15] contrasts the Johannine tradition with its resident president with the Pauline practice where an acephalous college of ruling elders is dependent on its itinerant apostle for direction and guidance. Perhaps we could draw a parallel with the Jewish traditions of colleges of elders under the Nasi in Jerusalem or Jabneh and resident apostles in Antioch, Rome or Damascus and under itinerant apostles in the smaller cities and towns. Although both traditions were strong in the early Church, the latter gradually gave way to the former which became the normative monarchical episcopacy.

F. Conclusion

G. Williams [16] delineates three general forms of the New Testament ministry. First, the inspired apostle, evangelist, proph-

---

14. *The Shape of the Liturgy,* Westminster, Dacre, 1949, p. 28.

15. *Les fonctions ecclésiales aux deux primiers siècles,* Paris, Desclee de Brouwer, 1956, pp. 163-174.

16. "Ministry of the Ante-Nicene Church" in *The Ministry in Historical Perspectives,* H. Niebuhr & D. Williams, eds., N.Y., Harper & Bros., 1956, p. 27.

et and teacher; secondly, the cultual and eleemosynary services of the presidents, deacons and widows; and finally, the disciplinary and judiciary and administrative offices of the presbyters from whom the guardians were drawn.

Modeled on their Jewish contemporaries, the Christian presbyters can be found in Jerusalem under the "Nasi" James, collecting and distributing alms to the needy, sharing with the Twelve decisions and judgments not only for the Jerusalem community, but for the diaspora as well, to which they dispatch apostles to promulgate their regulations. Paul and Barnabas go around the diaspora appointing ruling and judging presbyters with whom Paul kept in touch by visits and letters of instruction.

In the Pastorals we begin to see a distinction between the college of Christian presbyters and their guardian president, who is the father of God's family and the steward of Jesus Christ. Although presbyters seem to have been in the Church from the beginning, the guardians do not appear till Ephesus in 58. The distinction between presbyters and guardians is growing, but not yet is there the monarchical trend of the second century.

Presbyter-guardians must be morally upright and show the qualities of prudent government illustrated by the loyal father of a Christian family. They must be good and faithful stewards of the heavenly treasure left in their trust by the Master. Presbyters should be chosen with care, corrected when erring, and recompensed especially when engaged in preaching and teaching.

Christian elders as their Jewish counterparts were ordained by a laying on of hands to judge and rule the community in synod. The Christian elders appear to have been chosen by the Christian apostle, but not without consultation. It would seem that they held the places of honor in the liturgy as their Jewish confreres.

As yet we have no Christian priesthood paralleling that

of the temple. In the Epistle to the Hebrews Jesus is the sole high priest of his priestly people.[17] Not till the second and third centuries do we find priestly analogies applied to the Christian officers, first to the bishops, then to the presbyters and deacons.

---

17. As Jungmann writes (*The Place of Christ in Liturgical Prayer,* tr., A. Peeler, Staten Island, Alba House, 1965, p. 148), "The functions of a *hierous* as commonly accepted by the Jews and pagans of the time were simply not met with by the Christians in their presbyters. The Jewish priest in virtue of his divine commission, prayed, sacrificed, and expounded the Law, and was truly a mediator between God and Israel. The priest of the Hellenistic pagans, who served a particular shrine, where he had to ascertain the will of the deity and foretell the future, was likewise an independent middle man between the deity and the people. Both were regarded as mediators on account of their personal position and dignity. It was their special talent with which they tried to win God's benevolence. In Christianity, on the other hand, there was no human person exercising an independent mediation between heaven and earth. Here only Christ could be called *hierous* and *archiereus,* and he was eminently worthy of the title, since he alone has a sacrifice to offer worthy of God. What the Christian presbyters do, they do only as his instruments and in his name."

CHAPTER III

PROPHETS AND PRESBYTERS OF THE
SECOND CENTURY

As we move beyond the New Testament, we find forms of church government becoming more sharply delineated. Names such as guardians, presbyters and deacons which once were descriptive, now become specialized offices. Yet some overlapping remains for guardians and presbyters are still sometimes used interchangeably. Moreover, the charismatic ministry of the apostle-prophets is still very much a part of the picture.

A. Clement of Rome [d. c. 97]

Clement is important to our study of the early Christian presbyters. As the third successor of Peter and Paul in Rome he gives us significant testimony about the Roman clergy and those of the missions. He may have been ordained by Peter and served in the Roman presbyterate.[1] He probably was bishop of Rome from 90 to 97. Flourishing in Rome at the end of the first century, he is a fitting introduction to the second century ministry.

It seems that at this period Corinth is still under Rome as it was in the days of Paul. At any rate Clement feels free to admonish the Corinthians as his predecessors had done. Certain people in Corinth had incited the faithful against their presbyters whom in former days they had respected and obeyed (1:3). Now they had even gone so far as to depose some from office. It would seem that at this time Corinth is still ruled by an acephalous college of presbyters, dependent on an itinerant apostle, who may have been Clement.

Clement told the Corinthians that Jesus himself had foreseen jealousies and envy over places in his kingdom. As Moses chose Aaron to carry on the priestly functions of Israel (Nm 17), so the apostles appointed presbyters to take over the Christian ministry in their place, giving them a permanent character to pass on to their successors. With their tradition going back to Paul, himself, the Corinthian presbyters are to be treated with the highest respect.

> Those, therefore, who were appointed by them or afterwards by other reputable men with the consent of the whole Church, who in humility have ministered to the flock of Christ blamelessly, quietly and unselfishly, and have long been approved by all — these men we consider are being unjustly removed from their ministry. Surely we will be guilty of no small sin if we thrust out of the office of bishop those who have offered the gifts in a blameless and holy

---

1. Tertullian, *De Praescriptione*, 32.

fashion. Blessed indeed are the presbyters who have already passed on, who had a fruitful and perfect departure, for they need not be concerned lest someone remove them from the place established for them. But you, we observe, have removed some who were conducting themselves well from the ministry they have irreproachably honored. (44: 3-6) (AF 2, 74)

These ruling elder guardians of the church of Corinth can trace their laying on of hands back to Paul. Yet instead of the double honor due to them for an office properly fulfilled, they had been removed from the presbyterate. The guardianship (*episkopē*), far from being an occasion of strife, should be a center of unity in place of Christ, so that any one who rejects them, rejects him. Those men who are prone to sedition should leave the community so that the flock of Christ may live together in peace with its elders (54). In the Pauline tradition, guardians and elders seem to have been used interchangeably in referring to the church leaders of Corinth, while the ministering deacons handled the lesser tasks (42:4).

The presbyters of Corinth seem to be still under the guidance of their apostle, in this case, Clement, based in Rome. Clement of Alexandria (*Stromata* 4, 17) calls him an apostle. Eusebius writes (*History of the Church* 2, 25, 8) that in the second century the church of Corinth still considered itself a foundation of Peter and Paul. Thus, perhaps the successor of the apostles in Rome would retain some direction of the Corinthian Christians.

In Clement we see some analogies of the Christian ministry with the priesthood of Aaron (c. 43-44). As in Judaism the high priest, priests, levites and laity are assigned their proper duties according to their respective roles, "Each of us, brethren, in his own rank must please God in good ministry and with reverence" (41:1). In Jerusalem the sacrifice is inspected properly and offered by the priests.[2] So Christian services should be correctly conducted by the Christian ministers in a suitable place. Although Clement does not call the Christian officers priests, he does draw analogies which are the foundations for the later priestly presbyters.

Clement describes a developing ministry, not too far removed from that outlined in the Pastorals. The colleges of guardian-presbyters in Rome and in Corinth are under the Roman apostle who by his letters and perhaps visits gives counsel to the mission churches.

Hermas, prophet-presbyter of the church of Rome (fl. c. 140), has given us some interesting insights about the Roman clergy of his day. In his third vision of the Church in his *Pastor,* the aged woman describes the cooperation of the Christian ministers who are the essential stones of the tower of the Church.

> The stones that are square and white and fit their joints are the apostles and bishops and teachers and deacons who have walked according to the holiness of God, and who have sincerely and reverently served the elect of God as bishops and teachers and deacons. Some have fallen asleep while others are still living. And they always agreed with each other and had peace with one another and listened to each other. (Vision 3, 5:1) (AF 6, 46)

The unity of the church officers is necessary to the strength of the tower. Thus apostles and teachers are in rapport with the

---

2. Some say that priestly sacrifices continued in Jerusalem into the second century. See K. Clark, "Jewish Sacrifices in Jerusalem after 70," *New Testament Studies,* 6, (1959-60), pp. 269-280.

bishops and deacons, underlining the necessity of cooperation between the charismatic and administrative leaders.

The apostles and teachers are from the eighth mountain from which flow many springs watering all of creation.

> Apostles and teachers who preached in the whole world and who taught the word of the Lord reverently and sincerely and misappropriated nothing at all for the sake of evil desire, but always walked in righteousness and in truth, just as they received the Holy Spirit. The way of such, then, is with angels. (Similitude 9, 25:2) (AF 6, 152)

The charismatic apostles and teachers were important in the foundation of the Church (Similitude 9, 25:4), preaching in the name of the Lord and baptizing. But their leadership would pass to the residential elder-guardians and deacons.

From the tenth mountain are the episcopal pastors.

> And from the tenth mountain, where trees were giving shade for some sheep, are believers such as these: bishops and hospitable persons who were always glad to entertain, without hypocrisy, the servants of God in their homes. And the bishops, in their service, always sheltered the destitute and widows without ceasing and always conducted themselves with purity. (Similitude 9, 27) (AF 6, 153)

As the elder guardians of the Pastorals, these men should be good fathers of families whose homes are centers of hospitality and charity towards the needy.

In Visions Two and Three the role of the elders seems to point to a presbyterate in Rome, where they are honored with the first places (Vision 3, 1:7) and are entrusted with the sacred books.

> So you shall write two little books and you shall send one

> to Clement and one to Grapte. Then Clement shall send one
> to the other cities, for that has been entrusted to him, and
> Grapte will instruct the widows and the orphans. But in this
> city you yourself shall read it aloud with the elders who
> stand at the head of the church. (Vision 2, 4:1-3) (AF 6,
> 39-40)

This Clement might be the apostle of Rome and Corinth whom
we have already seen. Was he also the president of the Roman
presbyterate? At any rate Hermas stands at the head of the
church in the corona of the presbyters where he reads the
sacred books in the liturgy. Grapte may have been a widow
or a virgin (Similitude 9, 4:5-6), in charge of the widows and
orphans and working under the deacons (Similitude 9, 26:2).

Justin, the teacher-martyr (d. 165) tells us more of the
second century Roman church. In his dialogue with Trypho
he speaks of the Church as the New Israel, a priestly people
offering sacrifices through their priests. And in his *First Apology*
he describes the Sunday liturgy, where after the readings and
the president's homily, the bread and wine are offered, the
president giving thanks and the congregation assenting "Amen,"
after which the consecrated elements are distributed. The collection is deposited with the president for the care of orphans
and widows, the sick, prisoners, strangers and whoever is in
need (*First Apology* n. 67).

Justin was a Christian teacher, who, as his rabbinical
friends, felt himself to be the true successor of the prophets
of old (*Trypho* 1-8). The prophetic gifts remain now in the
true Christian teacher, just as false teachers are the heirs of
the false prophets. As the Rabbis did, so Justin lays his hands
upon the heads of his students who have finished the course
and are about to begin teaching. Although the guardian bishops
were to assume the official teaching chair of the Church, the
prophetic teacher has always had an important role in Christian
tradition.

B. The Didache

Although the *Didache* is derived from earlier first and second century forms,[3] its present edition dates from the mid-second century and reflects Eastern Christianity. It was used widely in Egypt. The *Didache* admonishes reverence for true Christian teachers, but not for those false teachers who undermine the apostolic tradition (11:1-2).

The prophets are permitted to give thanks as they see fit (10:7). Although the itinerant apostle-prophets are still in a privileged position, they will soon give way to a more stable type of residential ministry. Here apostles and prophets are taken together as in Paul and Hermas. "Now concerning the apostles and prophets, act in accordance with the precept of the gospel. Every apostle who comes to you should be received as the Lord" (11:3-4) (AF 3, 170). But if he stays too long (three days) or asks for money, he is a false prophet. When he goes on his way the apostle should be given bread, but nothing more (11:5-6).

But beware of the false prophets for not every one who speaks from the spirit is a prophet, but only if he behaves accordingly in the Lord. By his moral conduct, then, one can judge a true prophet from a false one for if a prophet orders the table to be spread and then eats from it, or if his actions do not fit his words, or if he asks for money, he is a false prophet (11:7-12). "And every prophet who has met the test — who is genuine — and who performs a worldly mystery of the church, but does not teach others to do what he is doing, he shall not be judged by you, for he has his judgment with God. For the ancient philosophers did similarly" (11:11) (AF 3, 171).

As the Jews of old supported their priests by tithing so

---

3. Chapters 1 to 6 may be based on an early Jewish synagogue manual for proselytes.

the prophet who decides to settle down in a community must be supported and also the teachers. Perhaps when the highly respected apostle prophets established themselves in a city or town they became the residential guardians of the local churches. At any rate they are revered as high priests (13:3) as the bishops were later honored. As the second century progresses we find more Jewish priestly customs and terminology applied to the Christian ministry, although it is not as widespread as it will be in the third and fourth centuries. The Eucharist is described as a sacrifice (14, 1-3) as also are prayers and offerings of the time.

In what is perhaps a later addition to the *Didache,* the author speaks of a more permanent residential ministry of the bishops and deacons, who, although they rank below the prophets and teachers, may replace them in the office of presiding and teaching. The use of the plural (*episkopoi*) might indicate a college of elder-guardians as at Ephesus in Acts.

> Appoint for yourselves, then, bishops and deacons, who are worthy of the Lord — men who are unassuming and not greedy, who are honest and have been proved, for they also are performing for you the task of prophets and teachers. Therefore, do not hold them in contempt, for they are honorable men among you, along with the prophets and teachers. (15:1-2) (AF 3, 174)

The *Didache,* then, portrays a two-fold ministry: the earlier itinerant charismatic apostles, prophets, and teachers and the later resident and elective guardian bishops and deacons. As the older missionaries settled down in communities, they may have been honored with the local high priestly president's chair. As the second century turns into the third and fourth, less is seen of the itinerant apostles, although the charismatic prophet teachers have always been with the Church.

C. *Ignatius of Antioch* [d. c. 117]

The second successor of Peter at Antioch, Ignatius flourished in the beginning of the second century. A contemporary of John of Ephesus, his fellow church leader in Asia Minor, Ignatius follows the Johannine structure of church government as resident president of a college of elders. It is in Ignatius that we first find a strong delineation of a monarchical episcopate, although he remains closely tied to his fellow presbyters and deacons.

Ignatius' letter to the Magnesians reflects a similar ministry there, with Damas as presiding bishop, Bassus and Apollonius as elders and Zotion the deacon (*Magn.* 2). Ignatius compares the bishop to God the Father and the elders to the college of the apostles, whereas the deacons are like Jesus Christ (*Magn.* 6).[4] Just as the Lord did nothing apart from the Father, either alone or with his apostles, so nothing should be done apart from the bishop and the presbyters (*Magn.* 7:1). As the twelve apostles gathered around the Lord, so the presbyters form a sanhedrin about the bishop (*Magn.* 6; *Trall.* 3), encouraging him and helping him to shoulder his burdens (*Trall.* 12).

Although the elders collaborate with and counsel the bishop, they cannot officiate in the liturgy without his special delegation. Ignatius, as the president of the Antioch church, has charge of admissions, reconciles, presides at the Eucharist and nothing may be done without his permission.

----

4. Ignatius refers to the bishop as the Father and the deacons as Jesus Christ, indicating the close rapport between the two offices. This analogy was used often in later literature. The apostolic presbyters, descendants of the local Jewish sanhedrins, may have been of less im-

Apart from the bishop no one is to do anything pertaining to the church. A valid Eucharist is to be defined as one celebrated by the bishop or by a representative of his. Wherever the bishop appears, the whole congregation is to be present, just as wherever Jesus Christ is, there is the whole Church. It is not right either to baptize or to celebrate the agape apart from the bishop. But whatever he approves is also pleasing to God so that everything you do may be secure and valid. (Smyr 8) (AF 4, 120-121)

In the liturgy the elders of Antioch sit around Ignatius in the traditional semicircle as a spiritual crown (Magn. 13). It is in the unified Eucharist presided over by the one bishop with his presbyters and deacons that the unity of the Church is centered.

Be eager, therefore, to use one Eucharist — for there is one flesh of our Lord Jesus Christ and one cup for union with his blood, one sanctuary as there is one bishop, together with the presbytery and the deacons, my fellow slaves — so that, whatever you do, you do it in relation to God (Phil 4) (AF 4, 101)

Anyone who sets himself apart from the unity of the sanctuary may not partake of the bread of God (Eph 5). The bishop is especially the center of unity when presiding at the communion banquet, breaking and distributing the one loaf and one cup (Phil 4). As the center of unity, the bishop has presbyters who are in harmony as the strings of a lyre. Thus the whole church sings in unison through Jesus Christ to the Father as a perfectly tuned choir led by the bishop (Eph 4).

---

portance in the Ignatian church, although the deacons at times seem to be under the presbyters (Magn 2, Eph 2, 2).

The *episkopos* should be respected as acting in our Lord's place, for he has placed him over his household (Eph 4). Christ is the one high priest and the bishop presides as his delegate with the other presbyters, deacons and laity sharing to lesser degrees the one priesthood of Christ. This is the body of Christ incarnate in the church assembled at the eucharistic banquet, surrounding the bishop and his presbyters in the communion of the saints.

In Ignatius we see an evolution of terminology. Whereas in the Pastorals and even in Clement *episkopos* and *presbyteros* are interchangeable and even *diakonos* is used as a general term for the ministry, in Ignatius *episkopos* is reserved to the president of the college of presbyters, taking the place of Christ. Although the sanhedrin of presbyters still serve as community leaders, they cannot operate apart from their president, the monarchical bishop.

Although there are a number of monarchical bishops in the Ignatian era, we also find the Pauline pattern of itinerant apostles and ruling colleges of elders. For example, when Polycarp writes to the Philippians, he does not mention a bishop, nor does Ignatius in writing to Rome. Perhaps Ignatius' constant insistence on the monarchical rights of the episcopacy indicates that this was not everywhere equally accepted and that perhaps the sanhedrins of elders were not always in complete unity with the bishop. As the age of the apostles came to a close it would be normal for the local presbyters to elect heads for this was the tradition going back to their predecessors the Jewish elders. Even in later times the presbytery would retain a voice in the choice of the bishop.

On his way to martyrdom in Rome, Ignatius stopped at Smyrna where he was hospitably received by Polycarp and the whole church. Later he wrote to Polycarp instructing him on the proper conduct of a bishop. The bishop should exhort all to be saved, unify the church, lift up all, be diligent in prayer, speak to and encourage all in God's example, be concerned with the sick, be gentle to the troublesome, prudent, sincere. The bishop should seek God as the pilot of a ship seeks the winds, standing firm against heresies (1-3).

The bishop must be the guardian of widows. As nothing should be done without his approval, so he should do nothing without God. He should not be haughty toward slaves. Husbands and wives should be married with his approval and with his guidance toward mutual love (4-5). The laity should be subject to the bishop with his presbyters and deacons.

Writing to the Smyrneans, Ignatius urges them to be united under Polycarp, their bishop, following him as Christ did the Father and to honor the presbyters as the apostles and to respect the deacons as the command of God (Smyrn 8). They are to do nothing without Polycarp's approval.

Polycarp, himself, writing to the Philippians lays down Pauline norms of conduct for the presbyters.

> And the presbyters (must) also (be) compassionate, merciful to all men "bringing back those that have erred" (Ezek 34:4, 16), looking after all the sick, not neglecting the widow or orphan or poor man; but "providing always for what is good before God and men" (Prov 3:4), abstaining from all anger, favoritism, unjust judgment, being far from all love of money, not quick to believe evil of any one, not severe in judgment, knowing that "we are all debtors of sin." (6) (AF 5, 21-22)

Presbyters should be kind and forgiving for they too will be judged, serving in fear and reverence, staying clear of temptations and false brethren.

Polycarp singles out one presbyter, Valens, who is unworthy of his office. If a man cannot control himself and keep himself chaste, honest, not avaricious, how can he recommend this to others? However, when he repents, he should be welcomed back with his wife and family as erring members and not as enemies, so that by healing the sick members, the body of Christ is built up (11).

Although in Ignatius and Polycarp we see examples of the monarchical bishop, nevertheless, in some places such as in Philippi the Pauline pattern of acephalous colleges still perseveres. Perhaps when the apostle prophets of *Didache* settled in these communities, they may have been honored with the presidency of the presbyterate.

D. *Irenaeus of Lyons* [d. c. 202]

A disciple of Polycarp of Smyrna, Irenaeus migrated to Lyons in Gaul where he became a presbyter of the church and later bishop in 140. The term presbyter for Irenaeus meant primarily those church leaders who knew the apostles, were their disciples and the guardians of their tradition. For example, the elders of Asia knew John the apostle who lived with them until the time of Trajan and delivered the traditions about Jesus to them (*Against the Heresies* 2, 22, 5). These elders who have sat at the feet of the apostles are to be honored and listened to. Frequently throughout his works Irenaeus uses the testimony of the elders or of a particular elder to back up his interpretations.

Irenaeus is the first Western author to apply the term *episkopos* to a monarchical residential bishop such as Ignatius of Antioch. A native of Smyrna, Irenaeus is a direct descendant of the Johannine tradition through Polycarp. Yet his stay in Rome under Eleutherius had placed him in contact with another tradition. Irenaeus describes the *episkopos* as a local church leader, instituted by the apostles and their successors so that the head of each community whether in Smyrna, Lyons or Rome is the true successor of the apostles and the guardians of the apostolic tradition. None outside of this tradition are to be followed (AH 3, 3, 1).

In the Roman church, founded by Peter and Paul, the

apostolic tradition is most perfectly preserved, for from these apostles has been an unbroken succession down to the present.

It is a matter of necessity that every church should agree with this Church, on account of its preeminent authority, that is, the faithful everywhere, inasmuch as the apostolic tradition has been preserved continuously by those (faithful men) who exist everywhere. (AH 3, 3, 2) (ANF 1, 415-416)

Irenaeus seems to use presbyters and episcopals interchangeably. For example:

It is incumbent to obey the presbyters who are in the Church — those who, as I have shown, possess the succession from the apostles; those who, together with the succession of the episcopate, have received the certain gift of truth, according to the good pleasure of the Father. (AH 4, 26, 2) (ANF 1, 497)

Avoid the false presbyters, serving their own lusts, not fearing God, contemptuous toward others, proud in their chief seats, living evil lives in secret for they will receive their just deserts (AH 4, 26, 3). Adhere to those presbyters who "hold the doctrine of the apostles, and who, together with the order of the presbyterate display sound speech and blameless conduct for the confirmation and correction of others (AH 4, 26, 4) (ANF 1, 497). Walking in the tradition of Moses and Samuel and Paul, they are the faithful stewards of the gospel, the true inheritors of the blameless, honest, and edifying apostleship of Paul. They preserve the faith in God the creator of all things, and increase the love of his Son; they explain the Scriptures honestly giving due honor to the patriarchs and prophets (AH 4, 26, 5).

The bishop, the chief witness and guardian of the apostolic

tradition, has the eminent right to the title of presbyter. Although the titles of presbyter and episcopal were often used interchangeably in the early days of the church in the East, in the West we find presbyter used as a special prerogative of the episcopal leaders. As the witnesses and guardians of tradition, they are worthy of great reverence, for these elder brothers of the Christian community, if they have not seen and heard the Lord, have witnessed the teachings of his apostles. When the eyewitness presbyter died, the title remained as one of reverence for their successors. The early heirs such as Polycarp were elders in the original sense of apostolic witnesses. Polycarp's successors, who had not known the apostles personally kept the title as second and third generation witnesses of the apostolic tradition.

So the tradition of the apostles is handed down by successions of presbyters in the Church. Yet some brash heretics felt that they themselves were wiser not only than the presbyters, but wiser than the apostles themselves, and so have discovered new truths that somehow escaped their predecessors (AH 3, 2, 2). Irenaeus taught the succession of bishops who held the esteemed title of presbyter (AH 3, 3, 1 & 2), successor to the apostles. Thus in his letters he calls the bishops of Rome presbyters as do some other church Fathers.

Although during the first and second centuries the term presbyter was applied to the Christian clergy often without determining an order of preeminence, yet this does not mean that there were no monarchical bishops, for Irenaeus who testifies to the existence of monarchical bishops from early times, uses the term presbyter to refer to himself and other hierarchs.

As Colson points out [5] we find in Irenaeus a convergence of two traditions of church order: the Asiatic Johannine and Ignatian practice and the Roman Pauline. But rather than con-

---

5. *L'évêque*, pp. 123-124.

tradictory, the two complement each other. The Pauline tradition emphasizes world unity in Christ who is the unique chief of the redeemed world without distinction of sex, status, or nationality. Thus the local churches are members of his body under the one head, Jesus Christ or his representative. Hence Paul's concern for liaison between the churches augmented by itinerant apostles. The West remained faithful to the Pauline tradition even after local monarchical bishops were established. When Peter and Paul died, many Western churches continued to be conscious of the successive primacy of the Roman church, the head of unity.

The Johannine tradition, according to Colson,[6] emphasizes the incarnation, the Word made flesh and united to man. Thus in each community Christians gather around the living incarnate representative of Jesus Christ, the center of unity. The local presidents who are called angels in the Book of Revelation or episcopals by Ignatius are the chief witnesses to the apostolic tradition guarding against false teachers and presiding over their communities in cult, court and service, surrounded by their colleges of presbyters.

So Paul's emphasis on the one body of the Church to the neglect of local autonomy is balanced by the local supremacy of the Johannine tradition. These still are the normal patterns in West and East today, although there has been a move towards decentralization in the West since Vatican II.

E. The New Israel

When in the year 70 the armies of Titus attacked Jerusalem, the rabbis fled to Jabneh, while many Christian Jews escaped to Pella. Thus geographically the Christian Jews removed themselves from the rabbinical stream, leading to the polari-

---

6. *L'évêque*, p. 124.

zation of the second century. The split widened in 135 when the Christian Jews refused to accept Bar Kokba as their messianic leader. Even by the end of the first century the Jewish patriarch of Palestine had ordered the malediction of the *minim* so that all dealings with them should cease and they should be excluded from the synagogue.[7]

Christians of the diaspora taunted the Jews with the destruction of Jerusalem and the temple for now all the messianic hopes and promises of the Old Testament passed to the Christians. Ignatius of Antioch echoes this sentiment when he says that if Jew or Gentile do not speak of Jesus Christ, they are nothing but tombstones and graves of the dead on which are inscribed only human names (Phil 6:1). Unless the Torah is seen as a preparation for the gospel, it is a mass of absurdities and unimportant details. The Epistle of Barnabas describes the Church as the new and true Israel of the new covenant with a new Sabbath and a new spiritual temple in place of the old.

Christianity must be the true Israel because Jesus fulfilled the prophecies and they cannot be fulfilled twice. The New Israel with its new temple, sacrifices, priesthood and ritual purity becomes normative in the third and fourth centuries. As synagogue terminology is replaced by that of the temple, elders become priests, and bishops, high priests. We saw the beginnings in Clement (c. 40) and in *Didache* (13:3) where the prophets received the first fruits as high priests, and in Justin (Trypho c. 117) where the Eucharist, prayers and offerings are sacrifices.

F. Conclusion

The second century of the Christian ministry was an era

---

7. See Justin, *Trypho,* c. 38; Origen, *Contra Celsum,* 6, 27; also J. Parkes, *The Conflict of the Church and the Synagogue,* Cleveland, World Publishing Co., 1961, p. 80.

of evolution. The free rule of the charismatic prophet apostle gives way gradually, but not without a struggle, to the permanent residential community officers. The bishop is raised to the presidency of the presbytery, although still called a presbyter indicating a basic equality. Successions of presbyter bishops hold the teaching office of the apostles and guard their tradition. By the end of the second century individual Christian churches are more sharply delineated: often there was a church in each large town.

A constant plea in Clement, Ignatius and their successors is for church unity against the threats and heresies and schisms. The bishop is the center of unity and should be obeyed as Christ obeys the Father. At this period the bishop is chief admissions officer, judge, teacher and cultic president. Presbyters, the advisors of the bishop and who can represent him in case of need, are to be honored as the apostles. At the head of his college of elders, the bishop teaches and guards the apostolic message. In the West the bishop retains his title of presbyter as a sign of his succession to the early apostolic witnesses. The Church of Rome is the true measure of apostolicity.

CHAPTER IV

PRESBYTERS BECOME PRIESTS: THIRD CENTURY CHURCH ORDER

The third century ministry continues on the road towards stratification. As the terminology becomes more priestly, continuing the New Israel theme with a further delegation of power by the high priest, the gulf begins to widen between the laity and the clergy.

A. *Hippolytus of Rome* [d. 235]: *the Apostolic Tradition*

Hippolytus, Roman presbyter, anti-pope and martyr, probably came from the East. His *Apostolic Tradition,* which gives us a good cross-section of third century Roman church order, was adopted as normative in the East, especially in Alexandria.

Concerning bishops, Hippolytus writes that the candidate is to be elected by all the people, indicating the still remaining democratic atmosphere of the synagogue. When the nominee is clearly pleasing to all, the community gathers on a Sunday with the presbyters and neighboring bishops, who place their hands on the head of the candidate, while the presbyters stand by respectfully. One of the consecrating bishops then recites the prayer, which reads in part:

> Thou who knowest the hearts of all, grant to this thy servant, whom thou hast chosen to be bishop (to feed thy holy flock) and to serve as thy high priest without blame, ministering night and day, to propitiate thy countenance without ceasing and to offer thee the gifts of thy holy church, and by the Spirit of the high priesthood to have authority to remit sins according to thy commandment, to assign the lots according to precept, to loose every bond according to the authority which thou gavest to thy apostles, and to please thee in meekness and purity of heart, offering to thee an odor of sweet savor.... (AT 3:5-6)

Note the heavily priestly flavor of the prayer. The bishop is the high priest of the community, serving, ministering, propitiating, offering the gifts, reconciling, and ordaining. After his consecration, surrounded by his presbyters, he gives thanks.

The people also had a voice in the choice of their presbyters, in whose ordination not only the bishop, but also the other presbyters took part. The bishop lays his hand on the head of the ordinand, the other presbyters also touching him, while the bishop prays:

> God and Father of our Lord Jesus Christ, look upon this thy servant, and grant to him the spirit of grace and counsel of a presbyter, that he may sustain and govern with a pure heart; as thou didst look upon thy chosen people and didst command Moses that he should choose presbyters, whom thou didst fill with thy Spirit, which thou gavest to thy servant. And now, O Lord, grant that there may be ·un-

failingly preserved amongst us the Spirit of thy grace, and make us worthy that, believing, we may minister to thee in simplicity of heart, praising thee (AT 8:2-4)

Here, too, in the ordination prayer of the presbyter, is a Jewish theme, but rather than the priestly refèrences of the episcopal invocation, we have the presbyterial tones referring back to Moses and the 70. Jewish elders also traced their lineage this way. Christian elders even at this date are the descendants of their Jewish predecessors who, ordained by a laying on of hands, were rulers and judges in a sanhedrin. Although called rulers in their ordination prayer, the Christian elders are losing importance, as the monarchical bishops grow in power. Despite their prestigious seats in the liturgy and their counsel to the bishop, their position became largely an honorary one, while the deacons took over the day to day running of the church in liaison with the bishops.

Did the presbyters at this time have any liturgical functions besides holding the honorary seats in the east end of the church? They are permitted to give the blessing at the agape if the bishop is not present (AT 26:11). At the Eucharist they impose hands on the offering along with the bishop (AT 4:1-2), and administer the chalices (AT 23:7-11). Could the presbyter at this time preside at the Eucharist in the absence of the bishop? In third century Rome the presbyters conducted the daily synaxes, leading the prayers, reading Scriptures and giving homilies, the Christian heritage from the ancient synagogue service. In case of need, no doubt, they were delegated by the bishop to preside at lesser Eucharists especially in rural areas. The bishop as president of the urban Eucharist, sent his *fermentum* to be distributed by the deacons to the lesser Eucharists of the smaller church gatherings, at which a presbyter presided, as his representative.

According to the *Apostolic Tradition* confessors are to be honored with the privileges of the presbyters, for by their confession they have fulfilled the main duty of the elders, namely, bearing witness to Christ.

> On a confessor, if he has been in bonds for the name of the Lord, hands shall not be laid for the diaconate or the presbyterate, for he has the honor of the presbyterate by his confession. But if he is to be ordained a bishop, hands shall be laid upon him. (AT 10:1)

Later this privilege was to be curtailed (AC 8:23).

The deacons of the *Apostolic Tradition* were of a different order. Directly under the bishop as his special aids, they had charge of property, finances, care of the sick. Since they do not partake in the presbyterate, they are ordained by the bishop alone. Whereas the college of presbyters was ordinarily consulted by the bishop, the deacons implemented the decisions of the sanhedrin. Deacons were literally the eyes and ears of the bishop in the community, letting him know who was sick, receiving the gifts in the liturgy, and if there were not enough presbyters, holding the chalices (AT 23-24). This latter custom was to lead to later abuses where the powerful Roman deacons held the chalices for the presbyters.

In the era of the *Apostolic Tradition* Justin's president or Irenaeus' presbyter-bishop is now the high priest, teacher and judge. Chosen by the whole local church and ordained by the neighboring bishops, he is shepherd, president of the liturgy, successor to the apostles and the guardian of tradition. As the progenitor of the new Christians he is called their father.[1] Although the bishop is still often called a presbyter, he is superior to his sympresbyters, whom he ordains, with whom he consults, and who surround him in the liturgy. The deacons are

---

1. In the third and fourth centuries "papa" was a common title given to bishops, expressing the filial reverence of their subjects.

his liaison with the people, his special liturgical and social assistants. Rome was divided into seven districts, each in charge
of a deacon.

Eusebius (*History of the Church* 6, 43, 11) tells us that
in mid third century Rome besides the bishop, there were 46
presbyters, 7 deacons, 7 subdeacons, 42 acolytes, 52 exorcists,
lectors, door-keepers, and 1500 widows. Under bishop Cornelius, presbyters headed local assemblies in the house churches
(*tituli*). In large churches where more than one served, one
was selected to be the chief presbyter.

B. Syrian Didascalia Apostolorum

This third century church order tells us much of the ministry
in the East. The author devotes chapters 4-11 to the functions
and qualities of the bishop. The bishop is the center of the
whole community, and holds the place of God in the government of his people. He is their high priest and king, an evolution
of the monarchical episcopal of Ignatius, with perhaps a more
Jewish flavor than the *Apostolic Tradition*.[1a] Bishops are the
high priests of the New Israel.

Then were first fruits and tithes and part offerings and gifts.
But today the oblations are offered through the bishops to
the Lord God. For they are your high priests. But the priests
and Levites now are the presbyters and deacons, and the
orphans and widows. But the Levite and high priest is the
bishop. He is the minister of the word and mediator; but

1a. For probable Jewish origins of the *Didascalia* see K. Kohler,
"Didascalia Apostolorum" in *The Jewish Encyclopedia*, Vol. 4, pp. 588-
594. The high priestly bishops of *Didascalia* (9), as well as the prophets
of *Didache* (13, 3) and the episcopals of the *Apostolic Tradition* (3, 5),
may reflect the high priestly Jewish apostolic delegates of the Nasi of the
time.

to you a teacher and your father after God who begot you through the water. This is your chief and leader, and he is your almighty king. He rules in place of the Almighty, but let him be honored by you as God, for the bishop sits for you in the place of God almighty. (DA 9)

The bishop of the *Didascalia* is a regal, almost divine person. He is the supreme judge of all with the God-given power of binding and loosing. Guarding the poor and those in need, he protects the widow and orphan, giving them alms which he has received from the faithful.

As guide, teacher, minister of God's word and the interpreter of Holy Scriptures, he has a right to sustenance from his people. The faithful should cooperate with him, letting him know what they do (DA 9). And they should never speak against him.

Through whom the Lord gave you the Holy Spirit and through whom you have learned the word and have known God, and through whom you have been known of God, and through whom you were sealed, and through whom you became sons of the light, and through whom the Lord in baptism, by the imposition of the hand of the bishop, bore witness to each one of you and uttered His holy voice, saying: Thou art my son; I this day have begotten thee. (DA 9)

The bishop should be honored for after God he is both father and mother to the Christian. He should be revered and supported as a ruler and king.

To be worthy of this honor, the bishop must be irreproachable, not less than 50 years of age and so removed from the lusts of youth. However, if a congregation is small, a younger man may be chosen provided he is mature, watchful, chaste, and peace-loving (DA 4). As the letter to Timothy recommends (1 Tim 3:2-4) the bishop should be a family man.

But it is required that the bishop be thus: a man that hath taken one wife, that hath governed his house well. And thus let him be proved when he receives the imposition of hands to sit in the office of the bishopric: whether he be chaste: and whether he has brought up his children in the fear of God and admonished and taught them: and whether his household fear and reverence him, and all obey him. For if his household in the flesh withstand him, and obey him not, how shall they that are without his house become his and be subject to him? (DA 4)

The bishop should be without blemish, without anger, merciful, gracious, loving, charitable to orphans, widows, strangers. He should not be a respecter of persons, not favoring the rich over the poor. He should be poor in his manner of eating. He should not be crafty, extravagant, luxurious, or pleasure-loving, not fond of dainty meats, or resentful, but patient in admonition, assiduous in teaching, constant in reading of the Scriptures, so that he may explain them properly (DA 4).

He should not love money and rather suffer a wrong than inflict it. Nor should he think evil of others nor bear false witness, nor be quarrelsome, nor love his presidency nor be double in mind or tongue, nor be given to receive slanderous gossip. As Christ he should be a model to his people. Finally, he should not be a wine-lover, extravagant or luxurious, but a proper steward of God's goods and not using them for his own gain. As the Levites of old, he should be nourished by the revenues of the church and not devour them (DA 8).

So the third century Syrian bishops must be family men of virtue as outlined in the Pastoral Epistles, which, no doubt, served as models for candidates for church orders. As high priest, father and judge, mediator between God and the faithful, president, the bishop dispenses alms, visits the sick, preaches, administers and rebukes. Nothing is to be done without him.

Little space is given to the presbyters in the *Didascalia* in

comparison to the bishops and deacons, indicating the prominent position of these two latter ministers in the third century
and the relatively honorary status to which the presbyters are
relegated. The deacons, the right hand men of the bishops, are
to attain a prominence that will occasion the strong reactions
of the Council of Nicaea, Ambrosiaster and Jerome in the fourth
century.

The presbyters of the *Didascalia,* in contrast to those of
the *Apostolic Tradition,* are chosen by the bishop. As in Hosea
(1:10) the king took from the people the ministrations required for the multitude of the people. "So now does the bishop
also take for himself from the people those whom he accounts
and knows to be worthy of him and of his office, and appoints
him presbyters as counselors and assessors" (DA 9). He also
appoints deacons and subdeacons according to need.

The presbyters sit in a special place of honor in the liturgy
in the east end of the church, a custom dating back before
Ignatius to the Jewish elders of the synagogue. "And for the
presbyters let there be assigned a place in the eastern part of
the house; and let the bishop's throne be set in their midst, and
let the presbyters sit with him" (DA 12). Presbyters and
deacons are to be present in the judgments of the bishop without respect for persons, as the Jewish elders sit in their local
sanhedrins. Reflecting Ignatian tradition, the bishop is as God
the Father, the deacons as Christ, and the presbyters as the
college of the apostles (DA 9).

At the community meal, perhaps the agape, food is por-
tioned out according to dignity. Thus deacons should get double
the portion of widows. And twice- two-fold should be for the
leader. The presbyters should receive the same double portion
as the deacons, "For they are to be honored as the apostles, and
as the counselors of the bishop, and as the crown of the church;
for they are the moderators and councilors of the church" (DA
9).

Deacons are more prominent than the presbyters in the

Didascalia for they are the official representatives of the bishop
to the laity. Finding out the needs of the faithful, they distribute
alms accordingly. The deacon is the hearing of the bishop, his
voice, heart and soul. When the bishop and deacon are of one
mind, there will also be peace in the Church (DA 11); since
the deacon holds the place of Christ, his relationship to the
bishop must be that of Christ to the Father. The laity should
not approach the bishop directly, but through the deacons.
"For neither can any man approach the Lord God almighty
except through Christ. All things therefore that they desire to
do let them make known to the bishop through the deacons,
and then do them" (DA 9). Deacons are appointed by the
bishop according to the size of the community, although seven
seems to be normative in many cities. In the liturgy one deacon
stands by the oblation, and the other by the door to observe
those that come in, afterwards they stand together at the offering in the church (DA 12). Deaconesses minister to the women
of the church, anointing them at baptism, instructing and helping the sick. They are compared to the Holy Spirit who according to Jewish tradition is feminine.

The triune God is reflected in the trinity of the Christian
ministry. Eastern tradition saw the Father as the monarch, and
principle of unity from whom proceeded the Son and the Holy
Spirit. In the third century Syrian ministry the bishop as God
the Father is the principle of unity of the Church, and his
fatherhood must be proved in a concrete manner as the head
and center of unity of his own family. Moreover, he is the
spiritual father of his community through the regeneration of
baptism. As a father it is his duty to feed, teach, guide and
judge his spiritual family. Representing God, he is the divine
voice to the community. In a manner analogous to the divine
processions, the deacons as Christ, and the deaconesses as the
Holy Spirit proceed from the father bishop to extend his largess
to the people of God. The presbyters of the *Didascalia,* as we
have seen, are more in the background, although as the twelve

apostles, they offer counsel to the bishop. How much a monarchical bishop used the advice of his presbyterate probably varied greatly with the individual hierarch.

C. *Cyprian of Carthage* [d. 258]

Cyprian's master, Tertullian, although originally from Carthage, may have been a Roman presbyter. In 220 he became a Montanist perhaps due to the high-handedness of the Roman clergy. Tertullian, in writing of the ministry, says that the bishop has the first right to baptize, next in line are the presbyters and deacons, but not without the bishop's authority (*On Baptism* 17). Tertullian's presbyters chosen with the approval of all (*Apology* 39), in union with the bishop may exercise the *sacerdotalia munera* (*Prescription* 41) that is, teach, baptize, and offer. Together with the bishop, their head, they sit as judges, as the presbyterates of old (*On Repentance* 9).

Even before 213, Tertullian seemed to favor the charismatic ministers, teachers and prophets (*spiritales*), arguing against those (*psychici*) who claimed that the days of prophecy were over (*Against Marcion* 4, 22). Whereas the bishops are the ministers of the Church, its true *imperium* comes from the Holy Spirit. All in the Church share its priestly character (*On Chastity* 7; *On Prayer* 28).

Cyprian, bishop of Carthage from 249-258, was a thorough student of Tertullian, although he presented a more balanced view of Christianity than his mentor.

For Cyprian, as for the tradition going back to Ignatius, the bishops are the centers of the unity of the Church, for upon the one episcopate is built the one Church. "The episcopate is one, each part of which is held by each one for the whole. The Church also is one, which is spread abroad far and wide into a multitude by an increase of fruitfulness" (*Unity of the Church* 5) (ANF 5, 423) (L 66, 8; L 68, 3 & 4). Just as a branch is fruitless when removed from the tree, and a ray of light taken from its source does not illumine, and a stream cut off from its source runs dry, so one who removes himself from the episcopal unity, withdraws himself from the Church.

The bishops succeed the apostles in place of Christ. Quoting Matthew (16:18-19) where Jesus gives the keys of the kingdom of heaven to Peter, Cyprian writes: "Thence through the changes of times and successions, the ordering of bishops and the plan of the Church flows on: so that the Church is founded upon the bishops, and every act of the Church is controlled by these same rulers" (L 33, 1 [250 AD]) (ANF 5, 305).

A bishop, chosen with the consultation of the people and the testimony of the clergy, was consecrated by his fellow bishops (L 59, 6; L 67, 4) and so inducted into the episcopal college (*Ordo Episcoporum*). The people of the community had had a voice in Cyprian's election as they did in Cornelius' and would later in the selection of Athanasius, Ambrose and Augustine. As the steward of God's kingdom, he will be held accountable for his service to the Master (L 69, 17; L 72, 3). "God commands a priest to be appointed in the presence of all the assembly. That is, he instructs and shows that the ordination of priests ought not to be solemnized except with the knowledge of the people standing near" (L 67, 4) (ANF 5, 370).

Cyprian often spoke of the priestly aspect of the Christian ministry (L 1, 1-2; L 43, 5; L 59, 5, 18; L 61, 3; L 67, 1; L 72, 2), indicating an increasing sacerdotalism. Since the bishops and their aids are dedicated to the service of the altar, all uncleanness must be avoided (L 67, 1). Moreover, they must refrain from worldly occupations such as the execution of estates (L 1, 1-2) (*De Lapsis* 6); as the Levites of old, they should be supported by the faithful in order that they may devote their full efforts to the ministry (L 1, 1). As so many of his predecessors, Cyprian insists that due honor be given to the priestly state. If our Lord respected false priests during his passion, *a fortiori* we should honor our true priests (L 3, 2).

Cyprian has a special warning for the deacons who had become powerful and truculent, to remember that our Lord himself chose apostles and bishops, whereas the deacons were appointed only by the apostles to help them in their work.

Bishop Cyprian ruled wisely for he often consulted with his people and his presbyters.[2] When several presbyters wrote for his advice, he was reluctant to give it for: "From the commencement of my episcopacy, I made up my mind to do nothing on my own private opinion, without your advice and without the consent of the people" (L 14, 4) (ANF 5, 283). He hopes to discuss the matter with all as soon as he is able to return.

In their ordinary duties Cyprian's presbyters have care of the widows, teach the catechumens, probably receive penitents in private (Pontius, *Vita Cypriani* 3). Moreover, they join their bishop in the public penitential court. Since they share in the bishop's priesthood (L 16, 4; L 61, 3), Cyprian delegates the eucharistic presidency to them in his absence (L 12, 1; L 16, 4). For example, the presbyters could offer with the confessors in prison, taking different deacons each time in order to avoid suspicion (L 5, 2). Also if the bishop is away, one who is ill and who has received a certificate from the martyrs, may confess his sins before a presbyter; or if there is no presbyter and the penitent is in danger of death, before a deacon. Thus experiencing the imposition of hands of repentance, they receive the peace which the martyrs requested in their letters (L 18, 1).

Since the bishop is the center of unity for the local church, any one not in union with him is not one with the church. In

------

2. The African Church preserved lay administrative and judicial presbyters called *"seniores laici,"* descendants of the Jewish presbyterial sanhedrins. Ranking between the ordained clergy and the laity, they were often consulted by the bishops as Cyprian did. See. W. Frend, "The Seniores Laici and the Origins of the Church in North Africa," *Journal of Theological Studies* 12, (1961), pp. 280-284.

a similar manner the unity of the whole Church is based on the unity of the episcopate (L 66, 9; L 59, 5). As we have seen, in time of need, the bishops can delegate their priestly powers. What was an extraordinary commission in the third century was to become ordinary in the fourth.

D. Presbyters of Alexandria

Clement (d. c. 215), who succeeded Pantaenus as head of the Alexandrian catechetical school, has given us some clues about the Alexandrian ministry. A contemporary of Irenaeus, he, too, speaks in the tradition of the presbyters who have safeguarded the apostolic teaching (*Stromata* 1, 1). As Irenaeus, Clement does not distinguish sharply between presbyters and bishops for the *presbyterium* is an honor to which they are raised together (*Stromata* 7, 1). The bishop is the presbyter to whom is given the first seat (*protokathedra*). At other times he makes a clearer distinction of clerical grades (*The Tutor* 3, 12; *Stromata* 6, 13).

In the Alexandrian tradition, Clement coordinated philosophy and revelation, philosophy preparing the way for faith by purifying the soul. Then truth builds a gnosis on the firm foundation of faith.

Clement writes glowingly of those who, even though not ordained, nevertheless, have presbyterial gifts by living righteously, gnostically and teaching the Lord's doctrine.

Such a one is in reality a presbyter of the Church and a true minister of the will of God, if he do and teach what is the Lord's, not as being ordained by men, nor regarded righteous because a presbyter, but enrolled in the presbyterate because righteous. And although here upon earth he may not be honored with the chief seat, he will sit on the four and twenty thrones judging the people, as John says in the Apocalypse (4, 4; 11, 16) (*Stromata* 6, 13) (ANF 2, 504)

Clement describes two types of Church service, just as there are two types of service to man, one aiming at improvement and the other ministerial. Just as philosophy improves the soul and children give ministerial service to their parents and subjects minister to their rulers, so also in the Church the presbyters serve towards improvement, while the deacons minister. "In both of these ministries the angels serve God in the management of earthly affairs. And the gnostic himself ministers to God, and exhibits to men the scheme of improvement, in the way in which he has been appointed to discipline men for their amendment" (*Stromata* 7, 1) (ANF 2, 523-524).

Clement distinguishes his Christian gnostic clearly from the heretical one who disdains the ecclesiastical tradition, the scriptures and the teaching of the apostles. "For us, then, he alone is a gnostic, who has grown old in (the study of) the Sacred Scriptures, maintaining the apostolic and ecclesiastical rectitude of doctrines" (*Stromata* 7, 16). Clement's gnostic minister, seeking perfection in knowing and loving God, seems to be of the charismatic order, as the prophet-teachers, confessors, and the monks of the desert, indicating a two-fold ministry, official and charismatic in Alexandria in the early third century.

Origen, Clement's student and successor as head of the Alexandrian catechetical school (203-231), more clearly delineates between order (bishops, presbyters and deacons) and the people (believers and catechumens). The bishop, elected by the people and the neighboring bishops, is the eye and right hand of the body of the Church (*Homily 7* on Joshua, 6). The savior of the Church, he offers to God the sacrifice of propitiation as the high priest of old (*Homily 5 on Leviticus,* 4).

The development of a strong monarchical episcopate in the second and third centuries led to certain abuses of power.

Perhaps reflecting his troubles with Demetrius, Origen writes that a bishop should be the servant of the Church, not its ruler (*Homily 6 on Isaiah,* 1), not misusing his powers to cut sinners off from the House of God (*Com. on John* 82, 4). Although he and the presbyters possess the chosen seats in the liturgy, they must live worthy of their station (*Homily 11 on Jeremiah,* 3).

Some clerics in their overweening conceit exceed the worst of secular rulers. Inaccessible to the poor, they are haughty instead of humble servants (*Com. on Matthew* 16, 8). Because of his high ideal of the clergy and his own hard fought presbyterial office, Origen criticizes those who struggle for the presbyterate for worldly motives and scheme to attain bishoprics (*Com. on Matthew,* 16, 22). Many clergy even simulate virtue lest their true unworthiness become known and so deprive them of their power (*Com. on Matthew,* Ser. 24). Still their unworthiness, though hidden, affects their ministry (*Com. on Matthew,* 12, 14).

Although the bishop is the prime doctor of the Church, correcting morals, explaining scriptures, the mysteries and theology, the presbyters share in this power (*Homily 13 on Exodus,* 14; *Com. on Romans* 2, 11). A doctor of the Church is not so much one who teaches in the Church, as he who teaches the Church, fighting against the heretics and the false doctors (*Homily 2 on Ezekiel,* 2; *Homily 6 on Leviticus,* 6).[3]

Although the local church (the city of God) has the same

---

3. Origen's ideal "doctor" was deeply spiritual, speculative, and a competent exegete. A descendant of the Gnostic *didaskalos,* he reflected a different tradition from that of the hierarchical priesthood. But by the time of Origen in Alexandria the teaching office was being absorbed into the priesthood. For this reason Origen had himself ordained. See J. Danielou, *Origen,* tr., W. Mitchell, New York, Sheed & Ward, 1955, p. 45.

name (*ekklēsia*) as the local political assembly, it is far superior. For example, the Alexandrian church is more stable than the *dēmos,* its council (*boulē*) is more virtuous and its *archon* morally above the civil ruler (*Against Celsus* 3, 30).

There seems to have been in Alexandria the custom of the bishop being selected by a sanhedrin of twelve elders. (Perhaps the civil archon was selected in a similar manner.) At any rate, the Alexandrian presbyterate seems to have been more powerful than that of other cities.

Jerome when writing of the arrogance of the Roman deacons (L 146, 1 *To Evangelus*) is witness to the Alexandrian custom of the presbyters appointing one of their number as bishop.

> The presbyters used always to appoint as bishop one chosen out of their number, and placed on the higher grade, as if an army should make a commander, or as if deacons should choose one of themselves, whom they should know to be diligent, and call him arch-deacon. For with the exception of ordaining, what does a bishop do which a presbyter does not. (NE 378)

Do the Alexandrian presbyters not only choose, but also consecrate their bishop? Ambrosiaster (*On Ephesians* 4, 12) writes that if the bishop is not present, the presbyters seal (*consignant*). However, the term "seal" is ambiguous. As we have seen, the evolution of the monarchical episcopal from the colleges of guardian-elders is shrouded in mist, especially since the terms presbyter and episcopal were often used interchangeably. It would seem, however, that in the first centuries of the Egyptian church, the elders chose one of their ranks to fill the episcopal seat (*protokathedra*).

Severus, Patriarch of Antioch who fled to Alexandria in

need, when they could baptize, reconcile, or preside at the Eucharist. Insofar as the presbyters are in union with the bishop and receive his delegated priestly powers, they become priests. Yet the deacons are still in a strong position since they are the chief representatives of the bishop to the people.

Other auxiliary ministers who developed in the third century were exorcists who had care of the insane and epileptics, subdeacons and acolytes who helped the deacons, lectors who read at the divine services, and door-keepers who kept unwanted intruders from the services. Since the bishops and deacons were completely occupied with the ministry, the laity should support them as the people supported the priests and Levites of old. Other ministers were self-supporting although limited to occupations worthy of their calling. Gradually the free rule of the charismatic prophet apostles gave way to the permanent teaching office of the monarchical bishop, although charismatic teachers still functioned as in Alexandria.

As the priestly aspect of the Christian ministry is emphasized, a growing distinction appears between the clergy and the laity (*Ordo et Plebs*). The old democracy of the synagogue, where presbyters were generally chosen by the people, gives way to the hierarchical ministry built upon the Roman model and analogous to the Jewish temple priesthood. Levitical purity and tithing helped to complete the image. As ecclesiastical provinces are patterned along Roman government lines, intraprovince synods discuss common problems and select new bishops. Certain mother churches held preeminence: Rome in Italy, Carthage in Africa, Alexandria and Antioch in the East. Rome has a special preeminence in the West as the apostolic see of Peter and Paul.

The third century liturgy is evolving away from its simple origins in the synagogue and domestic Eucharist. The daily synaxes of the presbyters and deacons included lessons, instructions and prayers. On the Lord's day the whole community took part in the Eucharist, presided over by the bishop on his throne at the back of the apse in the east end of the church, his corona of presbyters seated around him. The deacons bring up the offerings of bread and wine, placing them on the table; the bishop awaits, flanked by two deacons with presbyters standing behind. After adding the oblation, the bishop together with his presbyters lays his hands in silence on the oblation, followed by the bishop's eucharistic prayer ending in a solemn doxology and the people's "Amen." Breaking some of the bread, the bishop receives communion. The deacons then break the remainder of the bread on the altar and the presbyters break bread held before them on little glass dishes or linen cloths by the deacons. When the people have communicated and the vessels are cleaned, all are sent away "In Peace." The faithful often brought home pieces of consecrated bread for those who could not attend. After the third century deacons did this. Other deacons carried the bishop's *fermentum* as a sign of unity with the lesser Eucharists in the titular churches.[9] As the Church grows, the eucharistic presidency is increasingly delegated to the presbyters.

---

9. See G. Dix, *The Shape of the Liturgy*, pp. 104-105.

CHAPTER V

THE SACRED AND THE SECULAR: FOURTH CENTURY SACERDOTALISM

As persecution ceased and government patronage increased, fourth century Christianity grew rapidly forcing a restructuring of the Christian ministry. Synods and councils from Arles [314] to Chalcedon [451] set down canons that were to regulate the ministry for the next millenium.

By the Council of Nicaea [325] the old disciplinary and judiciary sanhedrins of presbyters were dissolving. The city parish (*paroikia*) expanded to what was later to be called a diocese, under the presidency of a bishop whose presbyters ministered to the titular churches in the city and to the neighboring towns and country districts. As the presbyters released their disciplinary and judiciary functions to the bishops, they gained in a delegation of the bishop's cultic presidency. Now both bishops and presbyters belong to the new priesthood of the altar.

A. Bishops

By the time of Nicaea the episcopate is distinct from the presbyterate. Canons from Nicaea to Chalcedon determined that bishops would be chosen by their fellow bishops of the province with some consultation of the people under the guidance of the metropolitan. Sometimes the emperor himself selected the candidate (Sozomen, *History of the Church* 7, 8, 3).

In the *Life of Polycarp,* written probably towards the end of the fourth century, the deacons are sent to the laity to inquire whom they would have as bishop. When they all asked for Polycarp and the whole priesthood assented, they appointed him. Then the deacons led him up to be consecrated by the bishops. The people still had a voice in the choice of their bishop, for Canon 18 of Ancyra [314-319] implies that if a bishop is not accepted by the people of his diocese, he must return to the rank of presbyter. Moreover, if he is dissatisfied with this and causes dissensions, he shall lose the dignity of the presbyterate and be excommunicated.

The synod of Arles insisted in Canon 20 that the new bishop be consecrated by a plurality of bishops:

> Concerning those who claim for themselves alone to have the right of ordaining bishops, we decree that no one take this upon himself unless he be accompanied by other seven bishops. If seven is impossible, that they should not dare to ordain without three others. (NE 325)

Nicaea (4) reiterates this canon, asserting that a bishop should be consecrated by all the bishops of the province. If this is not possible, at least three should consecrate, but those who are absent should give their consent in writing, confirmed by the metropolitan. As the fourth century progresses, more emphasis is placed on the episcopal choice of bishops, and less on the people's suffrage, perhaps because of abuses which had crept in. Chrysostom in *On the Priesthood* (3, 9-10) tells of those who sought the episcopacy for worldly reasons. Thus the Council of Laodicea (12 & 13) insists that bishops should be appointed by other bishops and not by the laity. In the *Apostolic Constitutions* (8, 4) the principal consecrating prelate asks the presbyters and people three times if the candidate is worthy. If the community approves his moral uprightness and his capacity to govern, he is consecrated.

As the Church becomes more structured in the third and fourth centuries, the wandering apostle prophets settle down in communities as ruling bishops. Yet since there was still a fair amount of wandering around, the synods attempt to keep bishops and presbyters in their proper places. To help settle jurisdictional problems, bishops and other clerics are not allowed to exchange dioceses (Arles 2, 21; Nicaea 15; Antioch 21; Rome [402] 13). Moreover, bishops are not to receive a person excommunicated by another bishop (Elvira 53; Arles 16; Nicaea 5; Rome [402] 16), nor interfere or assume episcopal functions in another diocese (Arles 17 & 26; Sardica 11; Rome [402] 15). And they should not persuade those of another diocese to come to their own in order to ordain them (Nicaea 16). However, Christian hospitality should prevail so that traveling bishops are welcome to offer sacrifice when passing through a strange diocese (Arles 19).

When a bishop is appointed, he must undertake the guidance of his diocese (Antioch 17) and take part in the synods (Laodicea 40). Accompanied by his presbyters, he presides at the liturgy (Laodicea 56). Keeping his private property separate from that of the church (Antioch 24), he should use the revenues of the church property for those in need and for his own necessities and not for his own personal gain. Otherwise, he is to be tried by the court of the bishops of the eparchy (Antioch 25). Although bishops are to be judged by the provincial synods (Sardica 3 & 4), they may appeal to Rome (Sardica 4). However, if the decision of the bishops is unanimous, it stands

(Antioch 15). Since the metropolitan has charge of the whole province, the bishops should counsel him and be consulted by him (Antioch 9).

Since the bishop is a family man, his wife and children should reflect his virtue. Thus his whole family must be catholic (Hippo [393] 17). Moreover he shall be strict with his sons, not allowing them to attend worldly plays or to marry heathens, heretics or schismatics, keeping an eye on them until they are of age (Hippo 11-13). A widow of a bishop, presbyter or deacon may not marry again (Toledo [400] 18). So the fourth century bishop is to be a model Christian and father of a family according to the Pastoral Epistles. However the trend toward abstinence in marriage and even celibacy was growing in this period as we shall see later in the chapter.

Fourth century legislation points up the jurisdictional disputes between early bishops and also the legal system ranging from the local courts to the provincial sanhedrin of bishops from which appeal may be made only to Rome. Supreme in his diocese, the bishop baptizes, blesses, reconciles, ordains, offers, deprives (AC 8, 28). But in case of necessity he delegates his priestly powers to his presbyters, except that of ordination.

B. Chorbishops

As the Church expanded away from the cities and into remote country places, some provision had to be made for the ministry to these rural Christians. Thus arose the chorbishop who ruled the country areas of the East especially in the third and fourth centuries. Although consecrated by a bishop he was not completely autonomous for he could not ordain without the express permission of the city bishop. Actually we find the equivalent of chorbishops mentioned as early as Clement (42: 4). And Eusebius (*History of the Church* 5, 16) names Zoticus a chorbishop of Cumane in Phrygia at the beginning of the third century. Since they were often in charge of remote areas, they tended to act independently of the city bishops, so that synodal canons sought to keep them in line. In fact, one reason that the chorbishops were eventually eliminated is that they presented a threat to the monarchy of the city bishops.

The chorbishops, modeled on the 70 disciples of Christ and ultimately on the 70 elders of Moses, are coministers of the city bishop, perhaps in a manner similar to the presbyters but with a difference. Because of their great zeal for the poor, the chorbishops may offer sacrifice (Neo-Caesarea [314-325] 14), but are forbidden to ordain presbyters or deacons outside their own parishes without written consent of a full bishop (Ancyra 13). When Novatian bishops were received into the Church they were sometimes made chorbishops so that there would not be two full bishops in one city (Nicaea 8).

Chorbishops, even though they have received the imposition of episcopal hands and are consecrated as bishops, should keep to the government of the churches under their care, appointing readers, subdeacons and lectors, but not ordaining a presbyter or deacon without the permission of the city bishop to which the chorbishop and his district are subject. If he goes against this, he is to be deprived, for he is subject to the city bishop who ordained him (Antioch 10).

The Synod of Sardica [343] (6) forbade chorbishops to reside in towns where a presbyter would be sufficient, lest the episcopacy be minimized by the smallness of the place. Laodicea (57) substituted for chorbishops *"periodeutai"* or visitors who were presbyters directly under the city bishop. The chorbishops who were still living were to do nothing without the will of the city bishop. So as the fourth century progresses the canons are stricter concerning the chorbishops, gradually forbidding further consecrations and replacing them with presbyters.

At the height of their power the chorbishops were quite numerous, ruling from market towns over the adjacent villages administered by presbyters. When Basil the Great found 50 chorbishops in his diocese, he demanded that they give him an exact list of those under their jurisdiction and in the future to ordain no one without his permission (LL 290, 142, 188, 54). Gregory of Nazianzus found that the chorbishops were often inferior, ignorant, and incapable of their office.

Historically the chorbishops were a step between the high-priestly monarchical bishop with full power to baptize, reconcile, offer, and ordain and the priestly presbyter with delegated powers from the bishop to baptize, reconcile, preside at the lesser Eucharists, but not to ordain. The independence of the rural bishops and their power to ordain seemed a threat to the power of the city bishops so that many fourth century canons were aimed at limiting their right to ordain.

There is little trace of chorbishops in the West, although Isidore (*De Eccl. Off.* 2, 3) describes some itinerant clergy of his time who appear to be similar to chorbishops. They were eventually brought under control by the Carolingian reforms. Morinus (*De Sacr. Ord.* 5, 6) calls them presbyters, although they seem to be between presbyters and bishops in dignity. Reflecting Moses' 70 elders, they are ordained by one bishop to act as his counsel, but cannot ordain.

C. Impudent Deacons

The deacons were important men in the third and fourth century Church. As the chief liaisons between the bishop and the people, they had constant contact with the laity: distributing the dole to widows and orphans, receiving strangers, visiting the sick, serving as auxiliary officers in the liturgy, and in charge of cemeteries and church temporalities. The seven deacons of Rome had charge of the seven districts of the city; their leader, the archdeacon, sometimes became pope.

Meanwhile the presbyters, as we have seen, slipped into a more or less honorary position, although still sometimes consulted by the bishop, near whom they sat in the church, and whose delegates they were in times of necessity. Yet in the daily running of the church, they remained in the background. In this light it was a normal reaction for the deacons to consider themselves superior to the presbyters, leading to certain abuses which the synods and Fathers of the fourth century tried to counteract. When they were finished the diaconate was relegated to the final step in the ladder to the presbyterate (*ordo promotionis*).

In case of need, if the bishop or a presbyter were not present, a deacon could baptize, but the baptism should be completed by the bishop's *cheirotonia* or confirmation (Elvira 77). However, in the persecution of Diocletian, when the bishop and many presbyters were in prison, some deacons had presumed to offer the Eucharist, a practice which was condemned by the Synod of Arles (15).[1] Moreover, the deacons should do nothing, neither baptizing nor preaching without the knowledge of the presbyters (Arles 18).

Nicaea (18) reacted strongly to the presumptions of the deacons, who in some places put themselves ahead of the presbyters and sometimes were contemptuous even of the bishop.

It has come to the knowledge of the Holy Synod that in certain places and cities the deacons give the Eucharist to the presbyters, whereas neither canon nor custom allows that they who have no authority to offer should give the Body of Christ to those who do offer. It has also been made known that now some of the deacons receive the Eucharist even before the bishops. Let all such practices be done away and let the deacons keep within their proper bounds, knowing that they are the ministers of the bishop and inferior to the presbyters. Let them therefore receive

---

1. See also Ambrose, *On the Duties of Ministers,* 1, 41, 204 (PL 16, 90).

the Eucharist according to their order after the presbyters, either the bishop or presbyter administering it to them. Further the deacons are not allowed to sit among the presbyters, for this is done contrary to the canon and due order. But if any one after this will not obey, let him be put out of the diaconate. (NE 363)

Justin (*Apol.* 1, 65, 67) had described the deacons' administration of the Eucharist, and in the *Apostolic Constitutions* (8, 13), they hold the chalices. Yet in their arrogance they often gave the Eucharist even to the presbyters, who could offer in the absence of the bishop. It seems that these deacons communicated themselves first, taking precedence over the presbyters and even over a bishop if he were not presiding (Hefele 1, 429). Moreover, they presumed to sit in the presbyterial seats of honor on either side of the episcopal chair. Although Nicaea went far to reestablish the honor of the presbyterate, Church Fathers felt the need to continue the struggle against the truculent ministers.

Ambrosiaster who lived under the powerful Roman deacons and who saw two of them, Damasus and Ursinus, struggling for the bishop's chair, wrote against the presumption of the deacons. He argues that in the early church bishops and presbyters were identical, with the deacons in a lower grade (*On 1 Tim* 3:10). So the deacons of Rome should realize their humble status and not seek to place themselves ahead of the presbyters.

Jerome, eminent fourth century sacerdotalist, also criticized the Roman deacons for assuming the places of their superiors (L 85). In his letter to Evangelus (L 146) he writes:

I hear that a certain person has broken out into so great a madness as to place deacons before presbyters, that is, bishops. For when the apostle plainly teaches that presbyters and bishops are the same, what happens to the server of tables and widows that he sets himself up arrogantly over those at whose prayers the body and blood of Christ are made. (NE 378)

Jerome, as Ambrosiaster, strongly asserts the dignity of the presbyters from the history of the early church. In the order of promotion deacons become presbyters, not vice versa. In an analogy with the Old Testament priesthood Jerome compares the bishop, presbyters and deacons to Aaron, his sons, and the Levites. In fact, there is nothing the bishop does that the presbyter cannot do except ordain (*ibid.*). Deacons should keep to their levitical ministrations.

In the *Apostolic Constitutions* the functions of the diaconate are clearly outlined (8, 28).

A deacon does not bless, does not give blessing, but receives it from the bishop and the presbyter. He does not baptize, he does not offer; but when a bishop or presbyter has offered, he distributes to the people, not as a priest, but as one that ministers to priests. But it is not lawful for any one of the other clergy to do the work of a deacon. (ANF 7, 494)

The deacons are supported by tithes (AC 8, 30) as are bishops and presbyters and distribute eulogies to the clergy according to their dignity.

Deaconesses appear in the East during the fourth century. Generally from the upper classes, they took over many of the functions of the earlier widows, for example, helping in the baptism of women, visiting the sick women of the community. The Council of Nicaea (19) decrees that the Paulinist deaconesses who had received the imposition of hands were not to be enrolled among the clergy, but to be considered among the laity. Hefele (1, 433) proposes that the Christian deaconesses may have received an imposition of hands which was essentially different from that of the deacons so that it was more of a blessing than an ordination.

The *Apostolic Constitutions* (6, 17) describe some qualities of the deaconess: "Let the deaconess be a pure virgin: or, at the least a widow who has been but once married, faithful, and well esteemed" (ANF 7, 457). In the ceremony of the blessing of a deaconess, the bishop lays his hands on her in the presence of the presbyters, deacons and deaconesses, praying that as the holy women of old: Miriam, Deborah, Anna, and Huldah, she be filled with the Holy Spirit and cleansed from impurities, worthily fulfill her office (AC 8, 19-20). "A deaconess does not bless nor perform anything belonging to the order of presbyters or deacons, but only is to keep the doors, and to minister to the presbyters in the baptism of women, on account of decency" (AC 8, 28) (ANF 7, 494).

The Council of Laodicea (11) states firmly that female elders (*presbytides*) or presidents (*prokathemēnai*) are not to be appointed in the church. *Presbytides* may have been older deaconesses who had charge of the younger ones or they may have supervised the widows. At any rate, they are not to be ordained in the church, as the presbyters and deacons were. Chalcedon [451] (15) stated that no woman should receive the laying on of hands as deaconess before the age of 40, and then only after a strict examination.[2] If she marries afterwards, she is to be anathematized together with her husband.

D. *Priestly Presbyters*

Fourth century synods and Fathers called for a stricter morality among the clergy. As the priests of the New Israel and superior antitypes of the old, *a fortiori* they must be clean, pure and moral men of trust. First of all, any who have proved

---

2. See also CTh 16, 2, 27 (390).

untrustworthy in time of persecution are not to be admitted into the ranks of the clergy (Nicaea 10). The Synod of Ancyra (1) said that presbyters who had lapsed, but who had renewed their struggle were to receive honor due to their status, but were not to be allowed to offer, or preach or any other priestly function. Cathari presbyters who came over to the catholic and apostolic Church are to be allowed to remain in the clergy if they offer their professions of faith in writing (Nicaea 8) and may communicate with the twice-married and the lapsi who have repented and been reconciled.

Once ordained, the clergy should continue their high morality. And if any are found guilty of any immorality because of scandal and lewdness, they should not be admitted to communion even at the end of their lives. (Elvira 18). Nicaea (9) warned that if a sinner is ordained a presbyter, the Church does not recognize him as ordained, for the Church only vindicates the irreproachable. Crimes invalidating ordination are blasphemy, successive bigamy, heresy, idolatry, magic, etc. (Hefele 1, 414).

To insure the maturity of the presbyters Neo-Caesarea (11) recommended that they not be ordained until 30 years of age, for this was the age that our Lord began his public life of preaching and teaching. Also due to experience with backsliding clerics, the Church was suspicious of the *clinici,* those converted in the crisis of serious illness. These should not be ordained unless they have subsequently proved their zeal and faith and there is a shortage of more suitable candidates (Neo-Caesarea 12). Furthermore recent converts should not be promoted to orders lest they be puffed up with pride (1 Tim 3:6) (Nicaea 2).

In the fourth century we see a further delegation of priestly functions from the bishop to his presbyters who bless, lay on hands, but do not ordain, nor do they deprive, but only separate those who are under them if they are liable to deprivation (AC 8, 28). The eucharistic presidency was delegated especially to country presbyters, who, however, may not offer in the city church when the bishop or city presbyters are present. But if these are absent, the country presbyters may be invited to celebrate (Neo-Caesarea 13). The Second Synod of Carthage [387] ruled that a presbyter may not consecrate the chrism, or bless virgins, and he may only reconcile penitents when the bishop is detained and then only with his permission. Moreover, if a presbyter celebrates anywhere without the permission of the bishop, he will be deprived of his dignity (3, 4, 9) (Also Hippo [393], 30). The sharing of the bishop's priesthood with the presbyters is illustrated in the *Apostolic Constitutions* (8, 28) where the deacon is described as an aid to the bishop and presbyters who offer, and one who although not a priest, ministers to priests. As the presbyters move from their colleges to the service of individual churches, they partake more and more in the priesthood of the bishops, resembling the priests of old serving their local sanctuaries.

John Chrysostom [d. 407] in his *On the Priesthood* has given us the finest treatise on the sacerdotal ministry. The ideal priest is wise, mortified, patient, prudent, grave but not haughty, awe-inspiring yet kind, authoritative yet affable, not a respecter of persons yet not condescending, humble yet not servile, strong yet meek (3, 16). He should take care of the widows and virgins, be a good manager, hospitable, a just judge, and a competent preacher. Reconciling sinners, he should strengthen them in their struggle against temptation (2, 2-4; 3, 4-5).

John, as Jerome, Ambrosiaster and others, sought to show the basic equality of bishops and presbyters as illustrated in the Pastoral Epistles. "Between presbyters and bishops there was no great difference, both had undertaken the office of teachers and presidents in the church. And what he said concerning bishops is applicable to presbyters." Bishops are only superior in their power to ordain (*Homily XI on I Timothy* 3, 1) (NPNF 13, 441).

Moignt [3] notes that Chrysostom underlines the teaching and ruling offices. The priest has charge of teaching in public, exhorting unbelievers to the faith, instructing catechumens, unfolding the Scriptures for the faithful and strengthening them against heresy, drawing heretics back to the fold. The priest must excel as a preacher, striving to emulate the eloquence of Paul. Moreover, if he fails to seek a humble oratory, he does a disservice to the faithful (*On the Priesthood* 4, 4-9; 5, 1-3).

John was reluctant to accept the bishopric and high priesthood for himself. First of all he felt that his monastic life had not trained him to live as a priest in the world (6, 3-7). Moreover, he had seen many seek the episcopal chair out of worldly motives (3, 9-10). He also feared that the ministry in the world might remove him from the contemplation which he relished.

The priesthood of the New Law far surpassed its ancient prototype.

For when you behold the Lord, immolated and lying on the altar, and the priest standing over the sacrifice and praying, and all the people purpled by that precious blood, do you imagine that you are still on earth amongst men, and not rather rapt up to heaven. And casting away all earthly thoughts from your mind, do you not contemplate with a clean heart and a pure mind the things of heaven? (3, 4) [4]

Priests have powers that even the angels do not have, for ex-

---

3. J. Moignt, "Caractère et ministère sacerdotal," *Recherches de Science Religieuse* 56, (1968), p. 569.

4. Tr. by P. Boyle, Westminster, Md., Newman Press, 1955, pp. 40-41.

ample, binding and loosing, administering the baptism of regeneration and the eucharistic food (3, 5-6).

Gregory of Nyssa [d. 398] in his *On the Baptism of Christ* (PG 46, 581) writes of the transformation of orders. Through the power of the Spirit water regenerates, ordinary stones are consecrated into an altar, common bread becomes the body of Christ, oil and wine are sanctified. So also by the power of the same Spirit the priest is honored and separated by his new blessing from the multitude of men. Whereas yesterday he was one of the crowd, now he is guide, president, teacher of righteousness and an instructor of hidden mysteries. "And this he does without being at all changed in body or in form, but while continuing to be in all appearance the man he was before, being, by some unseen power and grace, transformed in respect to the higher condition" (NPNF 5, 519). In his *On Virginity* (23) he recommends that priests abstain from marriage privileges as in the Old Law, for in the priesthood one is transformed from the human to the angelic. Since the priest allies himself with the great High Priest, he is a priest forever even in death.

In the West, Ambrose [d. 397] wrote in his *On the Duties of Ministers* that the priest should be a model of Christian virtue. In his letters to priests he stresses the high dignity of the priesthood and encourages them in their difficulties and discouragements. The priest receives, at ordination, the gift of the Holy Spirit for the remission of sins (*On Penance* 1, 6-8). But rather than a delegation of divine authority or a supernatural power which the priest exercises in ritual acts, it is the Holy Spirit himself who forgives sins at the prayers of the priest. Yet he does not hold any power over the Spirit except the power of intercession (*On the Holy Spirit* 1, 8, 90).

Augustine, Ambrose's disciple, writing against the Donatists, insists on the perpetuity of orders, comparing them with baptism. Since both are sacraments in which a man is consecrated, neither can be repeated. So when schismatic priests are received back, they should not be reordained (*Against the Letter of Parmenianus* 2, 13, 28). The sacrament of giving baptism is not lost any more than the sacrament of baptism itself. Thus both have a permanent character. In a sense the eternal Christian priesthood now replaces its type the Jewish hereditary sacerdotal order.

In his *The Good of Marriage* (24, 32), Augustine compares marriage and ordination. Although marriage is for begetting children, even if this does not follow, the bond remains till death. So ordination is performed to gather the people, yet if any one is removed from office because of a fault, he retains the sacrament of the Lord once it has been given, even though it remains for judgment.

Although Augustine strongly disapproved of clerical misconduct, he had little patience for those who were hypocritically scandalized at the lapses of the clergy. Writing to Felicia (L 208, 2 & 3), he points out that as Jesus had foretold, there will always be two types of shepherds, namely, the true guardians of the flocks and those who seek the office for their own personal gain. Thus sheep and goats are to be found among the shepherds as well as in their flocks. Some lie in wait for a priest or a nun to fall in order to cluck, "I told you so, they're all like that." Yet when a married woman is found to be an adultress, they do not accuse their wives or mothers (L 78, 6).

Even though a minister is evil, his ministry is still valid. "A minister, therefore, that is a dispenser of the word and sacrament of the gospel, if he is a good man, becomes a fellow partner in the working of the gospel. But if he is a bad man, he does not, therefore, cease to be a dispenser of the gospel." Those who receive the gospel from these ministers are not cleansed and justified by those who plant and water, but by him who gives the increase (*Answer to the Letters of Petilian* 3, 55, 67) (NPNF 4, 625). Since it is Christ himself who baptizes, is the minister any good at all? "Ministering and dispensing the word and sacrament, he is something; but for purifying and justifying, he is nothing, seeing that this is not accomplished in the inner man except by him by whom the whole man was created" (*Ibid.*, 3, 54, 66) (NPNF 4, 625). Augustine's disputes with the Donatists helped him formulate a theology of the sacraments stressing their validity and efficacy apart from the morality of the human minister and underlining the permanence especially of Baptism and Orders.

Augustine's famous correspondent and noted fourth century sacerdotalist, Jerome, exalted the presbyterate, as we have seen, drawing from the Pastoral Epistles which indicate that presbyters and episcopals were originally interchangeable. In his letters he pungently criticizes the defects of his contemporary presbyters and points up examples of the ideal priestly life. For example, in his letter to Eustochium (L 22) he takes to task clerics who spend much of their time in the homes of wealthy patronesses, who are puffed up with pride knowing that their presbyters are dependent upon them.

> There are other men — I speak of those men of my own order — who only seek the office of presbyter and deacon that they may be able to visit women freely. These fellows think of nothing but dress; they must be nicely scented and their shoes must fit without a crease. Their hair is curled and still shows traces of the tongs; their fingers glisten with rings. And if there is wet on the road, they walk across on tiptoe so as not to splash their feet. When you see these gentry, think of them rather as potential bridegrooms than as clergymen. Indeed, some of them devote their whole lives and all their energies to finding out about the names, the households, and the characters of married ladies.[5]

---

5. *Selected Letters of St. Jerome,* F. Wright, tr., N.Y., G. P. Putnam's Sons, 1933, p. 119.

Jerome feels that one reason for the existence of these worldly presbyters, is the very system of popular elections to clerical office. Often the best qualified men are not ambitious or are repelled by the machinations of ecclesiastical politics. Moreover, many of the bishops who preside at the elections are anxious to please their wealthy patronesses or prefer to appoint their own kin (*Against Jovianian* 1, 34). The increasing use of monastic candidates and episcopal communities such as Augustine's at Hippo were to help improve the quality of the clergy.

In his letter to Nepotian (L 52), Jerome spells out the duties of the clergy, who are called clerics (*klēros*) either because they are the Lord's portion or he is theirs. So the cleric must possess the Lord and be possessed by him. And since the Lord is his whole portion, he will not need portions of earthly goods. Thus he should serve a modest table and not be a money-loving business man. Moreover, he should be prudent in his dealings with women, who rarely should be in his house. Some clergymen in search of trusteeships thrust themselves between mothers and children and spend their time waiting on the sick and elderly rich in search of benefices. A cleric's deeds should match his words so that his mind and mouth are in harmony. A priest should be obedient and respectful to his bishop as his spiritual father, for a bishop and his presbyters are like Aaron and his sons. Presbyters should be examples to their flocks and not lord it over them (1 Pet 5:2). Moreover, a presbyter should not fear to preach in front of his bishop, who should glory in the talent of his sons; on the other hand, he should not seek applause, but repentance, based solidly on the Scriptures rather than on showy speeches written to impress the unlettered.

In his manner of dress the presbyter should be neither ostentatious nor dirty, nor should he be greedy for money nor pride himself in his learning .He should avoid entertaining the worldly and those puffed up with uncharity, for it is far better to put your confidence in the Lord than in men. He should flee the love of wine and fast in moderation, and should not be angling for compliments nor possess tongue and ears itching for gossip. In visiting homes he should be the comforter in sorrow and not the guest of their days of prosperity.

In his letter to Heliodorus (L 60) Jerome describes Nepotian an ideal presbyter who regarded his office as an honor, not as a burden. He answered envy with humility, never spreading obscene rumors, preserved his continence, helped the poor, visited the sick, was hospitable, soothing anger with kindness, rejoicing with the happy, weeping with the sad, a staff to the blind, and giving food to the hungry and hope to the hopeless. Frequently watching in prayer, he was grave in character, but cheerful in looks. He lived the life of a monk at home, watching, praying, fasting in moderation, edifying in conversation. Even in small things he was exacting, keeping the altar polished, the walls and floor cleaned, checking to see if the doorkeeper was on duty, the curtain properly hung in the entrance, the sanctuary neat, and the vessels sparkling. No task was too small for him. Nepotian is the ideal presbyter, the opposite of the worldly, widow-visiting, money-loving clerics chastised by Jerome in his other letters. Probably as today, most of the clergy of Jerome's era fell somewhere in between.

From the Fathers and synods of the fourth century we can gather that the presbyter is emerging from his honorary status to a true priestly son of Aaron. Although the presbyter is still under the bishop, more and more the episcopal priestly prerogatives are delegated to him as the need requires. As the priestliness of the clergy is brought to focus, a great separation from the world is insisted upon.

E. Priests in the World

Whereas the early Christian ministers were generally self-supporting as their Jewish confreres, when they donned the

sacerdotal vestments, they gradually were removed from unworthy secular occupations and were supported by tithes as
the temple priests of old. Although the Synod of Elvira (19)
did not forbid bishops, presbyters and deacons to engage in
trades, it did prevent them from leaving their cities in order
to seek trade elsewhere. (This may well have been a cause of
the wandering clergy mentioned previously.) Rather a cleric
should send his son, freedman, agent, or friend to conduct his
business, while he himself limits his trade to his own province.
Any cleric who practices usury is to be deposed and excommunicated (Elvira 20), for usury implies that one is covetous and
has an inordinate desire for filthy lucre (Nicaea 17), which is
certainly not fitting for a priest. Others who were in occupations
unworthy of a priest are: players, actors, soldiers who served
after baptism, magistrates, and emancipated slaves unless their
masters were Christian (Rome [386] 3; Rome [402] 4-10).
Although the Council of Chalcedon restricted clerics from taking
over the affairs or property of others, it still allowed them to
pursue a proper trade or handicraft or farm for their own livelihood (3).

As the empire became more Christian, Roman law gave
the clergy more privileges.[6] For example Christian clerics were
exempt from service on the municipal councils (CTh 16, 2, 21 &
22 & 24 & 36 & 40).

Those persons who devote the services of religion to divine
worship, that is, those who are called clerics, shall be exempt
from all compulsory public service whatsoever, lest, through
the sacriligeous malice of certain persons they should be
called away from divine service. (CTh 16, 2, 2) [313]

---

6. Many of these privileges were shared by the Roman civil priests
and the Jewish patriarchs, priests and presbyters (CTh 12, 1, 21; 12,
5, 2; 16, 8, 2 & 4 & 13 & 14).

It seems that certain heretics were harassing the clergy by nominating them for this compulsory and onerous public service (CTh 16, 2, 1).

Roman law also exempted the clergy from paying taxes even if they conducted a business for their own livelihood. Why this privilege?

> In order that organizations in the service of the churches may be filled with a great multitude of people, tax exemption shall be granted to clerics and their acolytes, and they shall be protected from the exaction of compulsory services of a menial nature. They shall by no means be subject to the tax payments of the tradesmen, since it is manifest that the profits which they collect from stalls and workshops will benefit the poor. We declare also that their men who engage in trade shall be exempt from all tax payments. (CTh 16, 2, 10) [320]

The families and servants of clerics were also tax exempt (CTh 16, 2, 14 & 26). Since there was a danger of some being attracted to the ministry largely by these tax privileges, limits sometimes had to be set. For example, in Alexandria the number of the attendants to the sick (*parabolani*) had to be limited to 500 poor men (CTh 16, 2, 42) [416].[7] Two years later 600 were allowed (CTh 16, 2, 43). Due to much abuse Valentinian III [453] finally had to forbid clerics to engage in trade under penalty of deposition. In general, the Roman government tried to encourage the recruitment of the clergy from the poorer classes (CTh 16, 2, 17). And once ordained, they should not be visiting widows and potential deaconesses in search of benefices (CTh 16, 2, 20 & 27).

---

7. The *parabolani* also antagonized the establishment by their prophetic espousal of the poor and the oppressed.

Under the protection of the empire, Church properties increased so that the bishops were more occupied in temporal administration. To prevent Church holdings from being handed on to their children legislation attempted to limit the choice of bishops to the celibate (CTh 16, 2, 44; C. Just., 42, 1; Novellae 6 & 123). As their business activities were curtailed, clerics had to rely more on the support of the laity.

F. Pure Priests

From the beginning Christian presbyters were married as their Jewish counterparts, and, indeed, the letters to Timothy and Titus recommend this, although certain radical groups such as the Encratites and the Montanists demanded celibacy. The Encratites claimed that the only true Christians were continent. But as Schillebeeckx [8] writes, they did not so much attach celibacy to the ministry as to baptism so that as late as the third century in Syria chastity is called "The crown of baptism."

As the Christian presbyters and their episcopal leaders took on more of the sacerdotal robes of the New Israel in the late second, third and fourth centuries, bishops became high priests, the presbyters, the sons of Aaron, and the deacons levites. And as more analogies were drawn with the old levitical purity, the discipline of marital continence and ultimately celibacy grew strong especially in the West, which was farthest removed and perhaps less understanding of the Jewish traditions of priestly purity. Since the priests of the old Israel abstained from their wives during their period of service in the temple, *a fortiori* the priests of the New Israel should do so.

Tertullian mentions unmarried clergy of his time *Exhorta-*

---

8. E. Schillebeeckx, *Celibacy*, tr., C. Jarrott, N.Y., Sheed & Ward, 1968, pp. 27-28.

tion on Chastity 13, 4). (They may have been Montanists.) In Egypt Clement of Alexandria encourages a married clergy based on the Pastoral Epistles (*Stromata* 12, 90, 1). So does the Syrian *Didascalia* (4, 4), which teaches that a bishop should be a man "of one wife," which was frequently interpreted that he should not marry a second time if his first wife died, but probably originally meant that he should be a man very devoted to his wife. If ordained unmarried a cleric was not to take a wife subsequently. Except for the Encratites and similar groups mentioned previously, married clergy were the rule rather than the exception up to the end of the third century.

The Spanish Synod of Elvira (33) seems to prohibit clerics from having sexual intercourse with their wives and from procreating children. However, as Hefele points out (1, 150), the Latin wording of the canon seems to be defective (*prohibere . . . abstinere . . . et non generare*) so that it seems to order what it would forbid, that is, it seems to forbid clerics to abstain from their wives. Similar defective Latin can be found in canon 80. Although canon 27 prohibits extern women (*extranea*) from living with a cleric, but allows a sister or virgin daughter, it does not explicitly forbid his wife from cohabitation.

We have seen in chapter two the reasons given for a married clergy in the early church. First of all, since celibacy was not in the Jewish tradition of elders,[9] the ordinary Christian presbyter or episcopal would be married. Moreover, the family of the presbyter, reflecting his qualities of morality, leadership and hospitality, should be a model for the rest of the Christian community. Devoted to his wife, he should train his children

---

9. In general celibacy was not approved in the Roman tradition as well. In fact, social and economic penalties levied against the celibate and childless were not relaxed until 320 perhaps under Christian pressure.

to be respectful and obedient and make his home a hospice in which the brethren gather for the Eucharist. The ideal family life of the presbyters and episcopals is safeguarded by third and fourth century synods regulating the conduct of the children of clerics.

But why the change in emphasis from an encouraged family life to the restriction of the marriage rights of the clergy? Among other factors,[10] the growing priestliness of the presbyters is of great importance. In the early synagogue structure of the Church, married presbyters were not only allowed but required. But as the presbyters became priests, and the head presbyter a high priest, on the model of the Old Testament priesthood, levitical requirements of purity were insisted upon more and more. Although the Jewish priesthood was, indeed, married, the priests were forbidden intercourse with their wives during their period of service in the temple. As Hughes [11] correctly points out, this was not a moral purity, but a ritual one, separating the priest from profane activity and setting him apart exclusively for the service of God. In this sense a church or chalice is regarded as holy. This concept of the sacred is found also in pagan religions where it was not unknown for priests to remain continent while ministering in the sanctuary. If the priests of the old covenant abstained from their wives for a time, *a fortiori* the new priests offering the new sacrifice at the altar and temple of the New Israel should observe a ritual sanctification and purity far surpassing that of old.

The Book of Exodus was frequently quoted (Ex 19:22; 28:43) warning that priests who go near the sanctuary of the

---

10. Other factors were spreading Encratism, with its jaundiced view of sex and marriage, pneumatic Monasticism, desire of freedom to serve the Kingdom. Later primogeniture and the inheritance of Church wealth became a force.

11. John Jay Hughes, "Married Priests: Solution or Sellout?" *Worship*, 43 (March 1969), p. 137.

Lord should sanctify themselves. In Exodus 19 the Lord told
Moses to consecrate the people.

> Go to the people and consecrate them today and tomorrow,
> and let them wash their garments, and be ready by the third
> day. For on the third day the Lord will come down upon
> Mt. Sinai in the sight of all the people. (Ex 19:10-11)

So Moses went to the people, consecrated them and they
washed their clothes. He warned them further "Be ready on the
third day; do not go near any woman" (Ex 19:15).

The uncleanliness associated with the emission of semen
is delineated in the Book of Leviticus.

> And if a man has an emission of semen, he shall bathe his
> whole body in water, and be unclean until the evening, and
> every garment and every skin on which the semen comes
> shall be washed with water, and be unclean until the even-
> ing. If a man lies with a woman and has an emission of
> semen, both of them shall bathe themselves in water and
> be unclean until evening. (Lev 15:16-18)

The uncleanness of these emissions may well be related to
early taboos associated with life giving substances such as
blood.

On holy occasions (Ex 19, 15) and even in a holy war
sexual abstinence seemed to be the practice. For example, when
David asked Ahimelech, the priest, for bread for his men, the
holy man answered that all he had was the holy Bread of the
Presence, which the young man could have only if they "Have
kept themselves from women" (1 Sam 21:4). David replied,
"Of a truth women have been kept from us as always when
I go on an expedition. The vessels of the young men are holy
even when on a common journey; how much more today will

their vessels be holy?" (1 Sam 21:5). Since the priests abstained from their wives before eating the holy bread, the same was demanded of David and his men.

More and more levitical purity is required of the priests of the New Law, or at least their marriage rights are restricted. For example, the Synod of Ancyra (10) said that deacons could marry after ordination only if they had declared their intentions beforehand. Neo-Caesarea (1) ruled that if a priest married after ordination, he is to be reduced to the lay state, but is not excommunicated.

Nicaea (3) forbade clerics to have *syneisaktoi* living in their homes with the exception of a mother, sister, aunt or similar person free of suspicion. This ruling referred principally to a spiritual marriage with a young woman as a *syneisaktos, agapētē,* or *soror.* Needless to say, problems arose from this sort of arrangement.[12] The *syneisaktoi* are not the real wives of the clerics since they are forbidden to all, and even the rigorists allowed the minor clergy to marry.

Historians agree that Nicaea was interested in passing a law of celibacy.[13] The proposed law was opposed by bishop Paphnutius of Egypt a holy man who implored that:

> Too heavy a yoke ought not to be laid upon the clergy; that marriage and married intercourse are of themselves honorable and undefiled; that the Church ought not to be injured by an extreme severity, for all could not live in absolute continence. In this way (by not prohibiting married

---

12. Sometimes, perhaps under the influence of the Encratites, clerics mutilated themselves in order to live in peace with their *syneisaktoi.* See Socrates, *Hist. Eccl.,* 2, 26; Ap. Canons, 22 & 23; Council of Nicaea, can. 1. See also Cyprian, (L 4, 1-5).

13. See Hefele 1, 435ff; Socrates, *Hist. Eccl.,* 1, 11; Sozomen, *Hist. Eccl.,* 1, 23; Gelasius of Cyzicus, *Hist. Conc. Nic.* A fear of the extremes of Encratism may have influenced the final decision.

celibacy, for example, Damasus I, Sirilius, Innocent I, Leo I, Jerome, Ambrose, and Epiphanius.

Ambrose sums up the western position in his *On the Duties of Ministers* (1, 50), using the levitical purity of the priests of old as an analogy.

> You who have received the grace of the sacred ministry with an untouched body, an untainted modesty, to whom also all conjugal relations are unknown, you know that you must be sure of an unhindered and spotless ministry, which must not even be profaned by any conjugal relation. I have not wanted to pass over this matter in silence, for in many further-off places clerics have had children during the exercise of the ministry, and even of the episcopate (*sacerdotium*). Furthermore, they defend their behavior by citing the ancient custom, when the sacrifice was only offered at intervals. In truth, even the people purified themselves for three or four days in order to come pure to the sacrifice. As we read in the Old Testament (Ex 19:10) they all used to wash their clothes. But if their piety was so great in the time of the prefiguring, what should ours be in the time of the reality? Priest (*sacerdos*) and levite, learn what it means to wash your clothes, in order to present a pure body to the sacraments you must celebrate. If the people (of Israel) were forbidden to take part in their offering without having washed their clothes, would you dare to offer for others with a defiled mind as well as a defiled body? Would you dare to act as their minister? [16]

If the Israelites were so careful of purity, even to washing their clothes before offering a sacrifice which was only a prefigure

---

16. Quoted from *Structures of Christian Priesthood*, by J. Audet, London, Sheed & Ward, 1967, pp. 142-143. See also Ambrose L 63, 62-5 (PL 16, 1257-1258) *Exhortatio Virginitatis*, c. 4 (PL 16, 357-358).

of the true sacrifice of the New Law, *a fortiori* we who offer the new sacrifice of the altar should be purified of body and mind. If the Jewish priesthood which was a type of the Christian, abstained from unclean marital intercourse while serving in the temple, *a fortiori* should the true priests of the New Law abstain. And since their service is perpetual, their continence should be perpetual. It followed that if the Christian priests could not abstain, they could no longer serve at the altar as their Jewish predecessors. Needless to say, the Jewish priests' service was not perpetual, for they only served in the temple for limited periods. The only way the western Church could try to enforce levitical purity was by requiring celibacy for ordination and finally by declaring clerical marriages invalid in the Second Lateran Council [1139].

As we have seen, there was less stress on ritual purity in the East, perhaps because it is closer to the Jewish origins of Christianity. For example, although the Syrian *Apostolic Constitutions* forbid bishops, priests, and deacons to marry after ordination, they equally forbid a cleric to put away his wife out of a pretext of piety (can. 6). Although there were still married bishops in the East in the fourth century, for example, the father of Gregory of Nazianzus, and Gregory of Nyssa, yet there was a definite tendency towards an unmarried episcopate, perhaps because of the problem of primogeniture whereby for several generations a bishopric would remain in the hands of one family.[17] Gradually it became a custom to draw episcopal candidates from the celibate monks. The Trullan Synod [692] besides affirming absolute continence for bishops and the right of marriage before ordination for other clergy, forbade inter-

---

17. Thus Roman Law demanded celibate bishops (CTh 16, 2, 44; C. Just., 42, 1; Novellae 6, 123). There is also some evidence of voluntary continence in the East. See Socrates, *Hist. Eccl.*, 5, 22; Cyril of Jerusalem, *Catechesis*, 12, 25; Gregory of Nyssa, *On Virginity*, 23; Jerome, *op. cit.*

times they were encouarged to leave because they had spoken up prophetically against heresies and social and political injustice and so endeared themselves with the masses of the common people. "If any persons shall be found in the profession of monks, they shall be ordered to seek out and to inhabit desert places and desolate solitudes." [19]

Although forms of common life were known in ancient times among the Buddhists of India and the East, the Essenes of Palestine, and the Therapeutae of Alexandria, Christian monasticism had its beginnings in Egypt at the end of the third century in the person of hermits and anchorites of the desert.

St. Anthony, the father of monks, made an impact even in the West on men like Augustine. As the eastern ascetics, the desert anchorites tried to master the human body completely, sometimes by severe penances and asceticism, vigils, prayer, and readings from Holy Scripture, aiming ultimately towards a perfect union with the One God. The liberation of the soul from the body is, of course, not without Platonic and Stoic nuances. Anthony deserted the desert solitude only on two occasions, once to encourage the Christians of Alexandria in the persecution of Diocletian and a second time to aid the bishop against Arius.

Often Christians followed the prophet-anchorites into the desert for help and counsel. Some remained, eventually forming communities. Under Pachomius [c. 323] the first cenobite life developed with a written rule and a whole monastery structure. The Pachomians linked their monastic vocation with their Christian calling so that their new life was based on their baptismal rebirth rather than upon any special type of profession. Besides Egypt, Palestine, Syria, and Asia Minor saw the erection of monasteries in the fourth century.

---

19. CTh 16, 3, 1 (390), rescinded in 392. From *The Theodosian Code*, tr., C. Pharr, Princeton, 1952. See also CTh 9, 40, 16.

Basil the Great [d. 379] grouped his followers around him in Pontus. Although he soon left to be a presbyter and bishop of Caesarea in Cappadocia, his rule of the common life, became the basis of many future communities. Jerome, trained in the East, spread monastic asceticism to Rome especially among the women, some of whom followed him to Palestine. Monasticism grew in the western regions of Italy, Africa, Spain and Gaul. Some bishops such as Eusebius of Vercelli and Augustine of Hippo gathered their presbyters around them in a common life, a family of future bishops and church leaders.

In the Post-Nicene period the monks were the heirs of the prophet-teachers of the nascent Church and the confessors and martyrs of the persecutions. As of old, penitent sinners went to the confessors in prison for reconciliation, so now they go to the monks. As the charismatic prophets of the desert, the monks served as a counter-balance to the absolute monarchies of the bishops. Originally lay Christians, the monks became more and more to be considered as a clergy of a higher calling. Evagrius [d. 399] contrasted the "righteous" of the organized Church with the "perfect" of the monastery. And he felt that the monks should show special concern for those who had been excommunicated from the institutional Church. Denys of the sixth century would place the monks in a position between the people and the priestly hierarchy.

The monasteries were ruled by fathers (abbots) who regenerated their spiritual sons in their new life by a second baptism of penance, a new name and new clothes completing the change. Although tending towards an independent existence, the monks often cooperated with bishops some of whom were former monks as Basil and Augustine. (This was to become the norm in the East.) Many bishops encouraged monastic foundations in their dioceses, often appointing presbyters to serve as chaplains. The prophetic monks were to play an important part in the survival of the Church especially in the early and later Middle Ages.

I. The Triumph of Sacerdotalism

By the end of the fourth century sacerdotalism had become the ordinary mode of speaking of the Christian clergy, temple terms replacing those of the synagogue. Although vestiges of this trend go back through Cyprian to the *Didache,* it is not till the third and fourth centuries that the old words were rather completely replaced by the new, the Christian priests of the New Israel succeeding their Jewish predecessors of old. Since the pagan mysteries and priesthood were dissolving in the fourth century (C.Th 16, 10), there was no danger of confusing Christian ceremonies and terminology with those of the pagans.[20] No doubt the pagan converts as their Jewish forerunners still felt the need of a cultic priesthood. This may have been a factor in the increasing Christian sacerdotalism of the time. At any rate, Christian episcopals became high priests, presbyters became priests, deacons levites, the eucharistic banquet a sacrifice on a table that is now an altar in a sanctuary, the Holy of Holies of the New Israel. The priest of the New Law should keep himself pure of all uncleanness such as marital intercourse. And as the priests of old were supported by tithes, all the more so those of the new. Moreover, the levitical deacons should not presume the places of the priestly sons of Aaron.

Moignt [21] points out an increasing ritualism during this period, the emphasis on liturgical gestures overshadowing the ministry of the word which had commonly distinguished the Christian clerics. More and more the Christian minister returns to the form of the pagan and Jewish priest, as a sacred person skilled in liturgical rites, a mediator between God and man. Along with the increasing liturgy with its allegorical comparisons with

---

20. Sacral terminology was also borrowed from the waning pagan mystery cults, e.g., *hierologia, hierourgia, mystagōgos, pontifex, sacerdos.* See J. Jungmann, *The Early Liturgy,* Notre Dame Press, 1959, p. 158.

21. "Caractère," p. 572.

ancient rites and its use of scriptural figures and symbols, there is a gradual decrease in catechetical instruction as infant baptism grows and adult converts from paganism decline. Moreover, doctrinal homiletics diminish after the age of the great heresies and public penance is reduced with the increasing reconciliation by the monks. Gradually the Christian priest becomes more of a cultual functionary in his local sanctuary and less of a teacher, judge and minister of the word.

As we have seen, the Fathers of the fourth century such as Gregory of Nyssa, John Chrysostom, Ambrose and Jerome taught the sacerdotal view of the Christian presbyterate, the bishop as high priest, the presbyters, his fellow priests. As the Church of Constantine grew, the priestly powers of the bishops were further delegated to their presbyters. Thus when the authority of the rural chorbishops was limited, the presbyters stepped into their places, ruling the country churches, yet dependent on the city bishop. In the cities, titular churches under the care of the presbyters grew in number, the predecessors of the parochial system, while the delegation of the eucharistic presidency gradually increased even in the cities. Bishops chose their presbyters with the consultation of the people, while the bishops themselves, if not under political pressure, were chosen by the bishops of the province.

As sacerdotalism increased the gulf tended to widen between the clergy and the laity (*ordo et plebs*), the cleric and the world. Whereas the elders of the synagogue had been near the people, the Jewish priests were remote. Hence when the Christian presbyters assumed the dignity and otherworldliness of the Jewish priesthood, they tended to move farther from the world of the laity. Certain occupations were now unworthy of the cleric. The immoral, recent converts or *clinici* were generally not acceptable for the ministry. Worldly business and trading became less popular.

When the empire became Christian, the Christian clergy tended to become a part of the Roman governmental system, perhaps replacing the civil priests and pontiffs.

In fact, it seems that from the time of Constantine, bishops, priests and deacons had their place in the strictly hierarchical gradations of Lower-Empire officialdom. They rejoiced in the titles *clarissime, illustre, gloriosissime,* and in the insignia of their rank, among which were the pallium, the stole, the sandals, and probably also the maniple.[22]

Probably progress up the clerical ladder paralleled that of the civil *Cursus Honorum.*

Although the government of the local churches had always rested in the presbyterate under the bishop, as the Church enlarged, provincial synods of bishops and ecumenical councils judge regional or church-wide problems.

Presbyters continued in close rapport with their bishops as advisors and counselors. And although the bishop is still the chief admissions officer, eucharistic president, teacher, judge, reconciler, he delegates these powers more and more, as we have seen. All fourth century documents agree that the presbyter cannot ordain, and men like Jerome would assert that this is the principal distinction between the bishop and the presbyter. Although in the East confirmation is delegated along with baptism, in the West the bishops keep the ordinary administration of confirmation as a sign of their charge over the admission of neophytes.

As the delegation of the eucharistic presidency became more common in the fourth century, it came to be considered as the regular duty and privilege of the presbyter, a priest offering sacrifice at the altar. In Rome the bishop as principal

---

22. P. M. Guy, "Notes on the Early Terminology of Christian Priesthood," in *The Sacrament of Holy Orders,* Collegeville, Minn., The Liturgical Press, 1962, p. 101.

eucharistic president unites with the lesser Eucharists by the distribution of his *fermentum* by the deacons.

While the priesthood became exclusively associated with the bishop and priests, the priestly view of the whole people was lost sight of. Christians became used to assisting at Eucharists presided over by a presbyter. And by the fifth century there was little outward difference between the eucharistic liturgy of the bishop and that of the priests. The presiding presbyter with his assistants sits behind the altar facing the people, as the bishop with his deacons and other ministers and flanked by presbyters if present, presided at the central Eucharist. At this time except for the pallium and orarion there are no special episcopal garments such as the mitre and gloves.

In the West there seems to have been a quicker delegation of powers from bishop to presbyters without the intermediary chorbishops of the East. Deaconesses were more of an eastern development, and the teacher and lector seemed more honored there. In both East and West the priestly character of the Christian ministry is to be the norm until challenged in the West by the Reformation in the sixteenth century.

CHAPTER VI

CONCLUSION

So far we have seen the origins and evolution of the Christian presbyterate from its humble beginnings as an heir of the local Jewish governing sanhedrins to a full fledged priesthood modeled on the priesthood of Aaron with all of its privileges and obligations.

Jewish Presbyters

Jewish elders were a natural form of government which had its origins in early tribal rule, becoming more formalized with Moses' choice of the seventy elders to help him bear the burden of authority over the people. Ruling elders were influential in the monarchy and in exilic and post-exilic times when they served as administrative and judging bodies in the local communities. The Jerusalem Sanhedrin, originally priestly, then dominated by the Pharisees, had charge of the temple and its ministry. As the highest court and interpreter of the Law, it supervised the lesser courts in Jerusalem and in the diaspora, sending its apostles to spread the word and law throughout the dispersion. The elders or presbyters of the Jewish courts, chosen from among the wise and learned, were ordained with a laying on of hands. And although at least in Talmudic times the apostles from Jerusalem had a say in the choice of the diaspora presbyters, it was not without the advice of the people. These local presbyters, in turn, guided, ruled, judged, had charge of the synagogue in which they held the seats of honor. By the end of the first century many local sanhedrins consisted largely of rabbis.

Christian Presbyters of the New Testament

We have ample evidence in the New Testament of bodies of ruling and judging elders in the early Christian communities. Since many of the Christians were either born Jews or proselytes, this would be a logical form of government. In the *Acts of the Apostles* we find a sanhedrin of Christian presbyters and apostles in Jerusalem under the presidency of James, deciding the legal problems of the diaspora mission church of Antioch. It seems that the Christian apostles appointed groups of ruling elders in their mission churches, where they acted as judges and as a liaison with the civil government as their Jewish counterparts did. The Christian elders should be morally upright, devoted husbands and fathers who govern their families well, and whose homes are models of Christian charity. The apostles should be discriminating in their choice of ruling presbyters and not hesitate to correct those who have erred. A presbyter who rules well should be honored by his people and recompensed according to his dignity.

Although episcopals are mentioned along with presbyters in New Testament documents, often no clear distinction is drawn between the two, however as the Church grew, the term episcopal or guardian was reserved for the head of the presbyterate.

Two traditions of church government may be seen in the New Testament, the first illustrated by James, the brother of the Lord, as president of the Jerusalem Christian sanhedrin of elders, the pattern which was preserved in the Johannine tradition and which was to become normative in the Church by the third century. The second is the missionary pattern established by Paul in which the local college of presbyters remains dependent on the apostle for direction through visits and letters. Although the Pauline tradition was to give way to the Johannine, nevertheless a Pauline influence remained in the papacy of the West, whereas the East has maintained its Johannine tradition of independent monarchical bishops.

Prophets and Presbyters

After the first century, individual church offices grew more distinct. Gradually and not without a period of adjustment, the charismatic and itinerant apostles and prophets gave way to a resident body of presbyter-bishops and their ministers and ultimately to a monarchical bishop as head of a college of presbyters. Although the monarchical episcopate is strong in a man like Ignatius of Antioch, nevertheless, he continues to call himself and is referred to as a presbyter-bishop, the center of church unity, taking the place of Christ, and the guardian of the apostolic tradition.

As the prophet-apostles settle down permanently in communities, they tend to become the episcopal centers of the local churches. With the parting of the ways in the second half of the second century, Christianity is more conscious of itself as the New Israel replacing and superior to the old. For example, *Didache* describes the itinerant apostle-prophets as high priests who offer the Eucharist. Although the whole Christian community is still a holy and priestly people, the gap widens between the laity and their priestly clergy. The Old Testament tradition of offering the first fruits to the priests is recommended also for the priests of the New Israel.

First century trends in church government continue in the second. In the East the monarchical bishop such as Ignatius of Antioch rules in a Johannine manner with his sanhedrin of presbyters, while in the West Clement advises the church in Corinth in the Pauline tradition. Irenaeus merges the two streams. A native of Smyrna, he was conscious of the monarchical tradition of the East. Yet he also knew and respected the Pauline Roman tradition, honoring Rome as the true measure of the apostolic teaching.

Presbyters Become Priests

In the third century the power of the bishop increases. Yet traditionally a presbyter, chosen by and from the presbyterate, he still works in close rapport with his fellow elders. Although the bishop is chief of admissions, reconciler of sinners, and president of the liturgy, in times of emergency he delegates his powers so that a presbyter or even a deacon may baptize or reconcile, and a presbyter may preside at the Eucharist. Deacons sometimes presided, but the custom was never approved.

The deacons, as principal social and liturgical aids to the bishop, soon became powerful figures especially since their number was usually limited to seven. As chief agents of the bishop, they were in constant contact with the people while distributing alms, attending the church door or holding the eucharistic chalice. Meanwhile the presbyters were largely honorary functionaries, except in time of need when they were delegated the priestly powers of the bishop, but they never received the authority to ordain.

The lower grades of the clergy increased as the Church

expanded with subdeacons, exorcists, acolytes and lectors taking over many of the deacon's duties. In country places the chorbishops or presbyters officiated, but under the direction of the city bishops. Larger church government along Roman province lines encouraged provincial synods under the bishop of the mother church, discussing church problems, judging and legislating.

The Triumph of Sacerdotalism

Although in the third century the presbyters assumed the priestly powers of the bishop in times of emergency, it is in the enlarged Constantinian church that they lose their honorary status as consultors of the bishop and become sacrificing priests under the high-priestly bishop in the Old Testament analogy.

As the Constantinian church formalized its structures, bishops were now chosen and consecrated by their fellow bishops, with the laity having much less to say in the election of their shepherds. While analogies with the Jewish priesthood became the norm, the gap between the laity and their sacrificing priests widened.

The chorbishops were all but suspended in the fourth century for they had been difficult to control by the city bishops. Now more and more of their functions as leaders of the rural churches were taken over by the presbyters. The prestigious deacons were limited by Nicaea which insisted on the traditional order in which the deacons ranged below the presbyters on the clerical ladder. Ambrosiaster and Jerome were vehement in their criticism of the pretending deacons.

As the presbyters received more of the delegated priestly powers in the rapid expansion of the Church, more and more care had to be taken in their selection. *Lapsi* were not accepted, nor *clinici,* Novatian converts and neophytes only with care. Moreover, candidates for the presbyterate should be at least thirty years of age and of high morals.

The last vestige of an itinerant clergy was forbidden as local churches clarified their boundaries and jurisdictional limits. When they became priests, the presbyters had to separate themselves from the world, limiting their trading and officiating in certain public offices. As of old, tithing was urged in the support of the new priests. Levitical purity was required in the West, at first proscribing marital intercourse to those who served at the altar, then forbidding marriage itself.

Semi-annual synods of bishops assisted by their presbyters and deacons became the normal mode of settling problems in the province or in the whole church in ecumenical session. Often called by the emperor or metropolitan to fight empire disrupting heresies or schisms, the synods also served as higher courts of appeal, and their legislation was to become the ruling body of church law.

The New Sons of Aaron

In the New Testament we do not find priestly terms used of Christian officers who are heirs of the synagogue rather than the temple. Even in the Epistle to the Hebrews Jesus himself is not a son of Aaron, but of Melchizedek, the mysterious priest-king of the time of Abraham. In the beginning the whole Church thought of itself as a priestly people under the high priest, Jesus Christ.

After the parting of the ways in the second century, we find some priestly references in the *Didache,* Polycrates of Ephesus and Tertullian. As the New Israel theme developed in the third and fourth centuries, priestly terminology and practice grew in the Christian Church with the bishop as Aaron, the high priest, and the presbyters as his sons, whereas the deacons were levites. The Eucharist took on more of a sacrificial form along with prayers and offerings. Thus the Christian priest offering sacrifice at the altar is the true successor of the priests of the Old Law.

Gradually as the priestly people gave way to priestly leaders of the people, lay-clerical separation increased. And although the early presbyters may well have been elected for certain terms, now the priesthood of the New Israel is perpetual in lieu of the hereditary priesthood of Aaron. Now the presbyters are fully priests, removed from the world, dedicated to the service of the sanctuary, ritually pure, a class apart from the laity who are obliged to support their high priest and his sons. This was to remain the central pattern of the Christian ministry until the reforming trends of the sixteenth century.

Peripatetic Prophets

Since prophecy is very much in evidence among God's people today, it might do well to examine the early Christian prophetic ministry which preceded and paralleled the formal ordained and priestly hierarchy.

The concept of prophecy goes back to early Judaism. Before the monarchy groups called sons of the prophets were cultic functionaries, worshiping in song and dance. Often they engaged in political affairs as Samuel, Gad and Nathan, and Isaiah. Advising the king, the prophets had a special charism so that Yahweh spoke through them, as the Law was the charism of the priests and wisdom of the wise men (Jer 18, 18).[1] Inspired and motivated by Yahweh, the prophet is mystically transformed and driven to speak. Experiencing the presence of God, he uses the formula "Thus speaks Yahweh," threatening, promising, reproaching, warning, speaking with wisdom. In post-exilic times the scribal lawyers supplanted the prophets.

In the New Testament we find prophetic figures such as

---

1. Law and Prophecy, far from antagonistic, are parts of a whole in the Hebrew Bible. C.f., I. Abrahams, *Studies,* II, p. 125.

John the Baptist. Was Jesus himself a prophet? He is called one many times (Mt 16, 24; 21, 11 and 46; Mk 6, 15; Lk 9, 8), although he never applied the title to himself. McKenzie [2] writes that Jesus resembles a prophet more than any other Hebrew religious figure. He speaks for God, standing outside the cultic and political structure. But rather than using a prophetic formula, he speaks on his own authority. When the people try to identify him with the prophetic precursor of the Messiah, he rather points to John the Baptist (Mt 11, 7-10; Lk 7, 24-27).

Jesus fits into the rabbinic Pharisaic stream. The rabbis felt themselves to be the successors of the prophets by way of the elders of the Great Synagogue (*Pirke Aboth* 1, 1-2). Opposed to the hierarchical structure of the temple, the Pharisaic rabbis were synagogue-orientated and closer to the common people, thus constituting a sort of unofficial Jewish clergy. They strove for a perfect observance of the Law, interpreting it for the unlearned. The rabbi Jesus of Nazareth trains his disciples, sending them as apostles and prophets with his delegated authority to proclaim the gospel, baptizing and teaching the kingdom (Mt 23:34-36; 28:16-20; Lk 17:49).

Paul is a Pharisaic rabbi par excellence, although his diaspora interpretation of the Law was at odds with the Palestinian rabbis. Paul is numbered among the prophet-rabbis of Antioch (Acts 13:1-3). Sent as a missionary, Paul is an apostle, prophet and teacher, but always the servant or minister of Jesus Christ and the Church. Actually the charisms of prophet and teacher overlapped,[3] and when on the missions these men were also called apostles. In enumerating the ministries (e.g., 1 Cor

---

2. *Dictionary of the Bible*, Milwaukee, Bruce, 1965, p. 699.

3. As Abrahams says (*Studies*, II, 123), "The popularity of the canonical Gospels would render the prophet superfluous; preacher and teacher, unfolding, nay enlarging, Law or Gospel took the prophet's place."

12:28; Eph 3:5) Paul often gave precedence to the apostles, prophets and teachers. The apostles and prophets are the foundation stones of the Church with Jesus himself as the cornerstone (Eph 2:20).

In the second century Hermas described the charismatic apostles and teachers as essential building stones of the church tower along with the bishops and deacons. Justin, too, saw the Christian teachers as the successors to the prophets of old. Although the Eastern *Didache* honors the prophet-apostles (10: 7; 11:3-4) it also warns against false prophets who use their charism for material gain (11:5-12). When an elderly prophet-apostle settles down he is to be supported by the community as the high priest of old (13:3). Gradually they gave way to residential ministers (15:1-2), bishops and deacons.

Prophecy came especially to the fore in the Montanist movement of the second century. Montanus, a Phrygian, proclaimed himself as the one through whom the dispensation of the Paraclete had begun. Joined by the prophetesses Priscia and Maxilla, he preached the proximity of the New Jerusalem and the Millenium, to be anticipated by a celibate life. Visions, revelations, prophets and prophetesses marked an exaggeration of earlier (Johannine?) trends over against the Hellenizing tendencies of the times. Tertullian was attracted to the Montanists in 207.

During the persecutions, the confessors constituted a type of unofficial prophetic ministry and were honored as presbyters. Moreover, they gave letters of reconciliation to sinners.

Third century Alexandria saw charismatic gnostic ministers, who although not ordained, nevertheless, possess presbyterial gifts by living gnostically and teaching the Lord's doctrine. Clement's (*Stromata* 7:1) gnostic ministers, seeking perfection in knowing and loving God, seem to be of the pneumatic order as the prophet-teachers, confessors, and later the monks. The monks of the desert continued the prophetic line of the Church, so that sinners flocked to the desert for reconciliation. Although not ordained, they began to be considered as a type of clergy ranging in between the laity and the hierarchy. Prophetically they campaigned against injustice, for example, they often rescued prisoners whom they thought had been wrongly accused.

The unofficial prophetic ministry of the Church has carried on through the ages. Indeed, there will always be prophecy as long as there is the Spirit. Beginning as charismatic and unstructured, it tended to become formalized as in the monastic orders, reformation churches and pietist groups. Today more than ever before we are in a prophetic age, with apparent clashes between the formal and informal ministries. There is more and more talk of the underground church, of prophetic demonstrations against the establishment, of teachers in opposition to bishops, of liberals clashing with conservatives. Abrahams has stated well: [4]

> By the nature of the case, prophecy could not flourish unless the synagogue and the church were prepared to reconsider their attitude towards the immutability of the older revelations .... The liberal movement in Judaism is, in a sense, a return to the prophetic spirit ... because liberalism in religions places on the whole its chief stress and reliance on the direct power of great ideas, because in its statement of these ideas it is in a creative frame of mind.

Religions tend to lose their creative faculty, but prophecy returns as a creative drive.

The true prophet and the true ordained minister are often complementary and can be the same person. It is when either one or the other is false to his vocation that trouble ensues. Although we must be on guard against false prophets, neverthe-

---

4. *Studies*, II, 124.

less, even the true prophets are liable to stoning from the establishment, especially when preaching or teaching against a policy which although established may well be unjust.

Levites and Laity

The Jewish priests were physically perfect, consecrated and set apart from the people. Supported by tithes and ritually pure, they served in the temple for definite periods. At the time of Jesus they were often associated with the upper classes.

The Pharisaic rabbis, on the other hand, were closer to the common people in keeping with the more democratic atmosphere of the synagogue. It seems to have been the practice of local communities to choose their governing board of presbyters, who were then honored with the chief seats. Even if the Nasi or his apostle appointed them, it was not without consultation of the people. In contrast to the priests, the presbyters were self-supporting and in close rapport with their neighbors.

Christian presbyters came from the synagogue tradition and the people had a voice in their choice even though appointed by an apostle. Evidence of a lay-clerical split can be seen in the Pauline, Clementine, and Ignatian warnings against disrespect for the elders, perhaps brought on by envy of their first seats, or by haughtiness of some elders.

In general, early Christian presbyters and episcopals kept a close contact with the laity, who had a part in their election. As sacerdotalism became the tone of the third and fourth century Church, a greater separation grew between clergy and laity as had been true between the Jewish priests and the people. Now the Christian presbyters are priests, consecrated as a class apart, supported by tithes, removed from the world, and ritually pure.

More and more bishops are chosen by their fellow bishops and presbyters are appointed by the bishops with less consultation of the laity. Gradually the democracy of the synagogue gives way to the monarchy of the hierarchy, with less emphasis on the priestly people and more on the priests of the people.

Although Reformation churches were by and large lay-orientated and lay-controlled, it was not until Vatican II that Roman Catholic laity came fully into its own both in the liturgy and in church government through parish and diocesan boards with the priesthood now a ministry to rather than a domination of the People of God.

The Christian Ministry Today and Tomorrow

Today the Christian ministry is undergoing one of its most serious identity crises. Through the centuries Christian clerics have had their ups and downs. The Pastoral Epistles and the Fathers urge respect for the presbyters, implying that they were not always honored. In fact, in the late third and early fourth centuries they were often functionaries of less importance than the deacons. Yet the presbyters of today seem even less sure of themselves, judging from the drop in vocations and the increasing defections from the ministry. The ancient tradition of a sacrificing priesthood seems to be giving way to a social apostolate similar to that of the early presbyter-bishops and their deacon assistants. Does this mean a return to the synagogue and home-orientated ministry?

Certainly our liturgy has returned to earlier forms. The altar has once again become a banquet table; the presbyter presides, but the laity participate in the readings, offertory and prayers. A clearer line is drawn between the synaxes of the ambo and the anaphora of the table. If the ministry too, continues its devolution to earlier forms, the bishops will make increasing use of their right-hand men, the deacons. There will be less emphasis on the separation of the clergy from the world. Some may work at legitimate occupations during the week, while serving in the churches on Sundays or in private homes where they may preside at lesser eucharists. A new attitude towards marital intercourse, namely, that it is pure and good, will show its compatibility with the ministry. The presbyter's family, as of old, will be the community exemplar of unity and charity. The old collegiality of the presbyters has already been resumed in many dioceses where the bishop presides at the head of the presbyterate, which gives him aid and counsel in governing and judging.

The rise of the prophetic ministry echoes that of the early Church. Indeed, today's prophet-teachers, parallel to the established ministry, reflect a healthy tradition going back to Paul and Jesus himself, as we have seen. Yet the danger of false prophets is still with us. Are the prophets moral men, are they working for financial gain or personal fame, do they presume too long on the hospitality of others? These early criteria could well be applied today.

As in the early Church, the careful choice of presbyters is of the essence today. Family men of good morals, well-educated, capable of dynamic church leadership are badly needed on all levels of the ministry. Anti-clericalism has been with us since the beginning, witness the admonitions of the early church to honor the presbyters. But as of old, perhaps the lack of honor is due, at least in part, to the dishonorable conduct of the elders.

Perhaps today's deacons, as special representatives of the bishop will regain their former prestige. It will be interesting to see whether modern deacons overshadow the presbyters as their predecessors did. Deaconesses, too, may be of help especially in missionary areas.

Since Vatican II, the priestly people of God has come into a position of prominence alongside the presbyters, not only participating actively in the liturgy, but also in their own collegiality advising the presbyters and even the bishops. Although the distinction between laity and clergy is less than formerly, it is still in evidence.

Hoping to renew its early spirit, the Church of today is devolving to earlier forms of liturgy and ministry. As the laity, in general, has welcomed the earlier forms of the liturgy, freed from centuries of accretions, so, I believe, it will welcome a ministry which is at least in part removed from the temple and given back to the people, a ministry which is a part of the world, leading an exemplary and hospitable family life so recommended to the early presbyters.

But will there be no place for the celibate cultual priest representing Jesus as the mediator between man and God? There seems to be a basic need in man for a ceremonial priesthood. The Jews, Greeks and Romans had it and when they became Christians they still needed and wanted it. This author feels that although the Christian ministry may well move in the direction of a simplified, social-minded, Word-centered service, man will always seek a ritual, sacrificial, a holy and sacred and cultic priesthood apart from the world, interceding, propitiating, offering at the altar of God in lieu of Christ the High Priest. Although this may play a decreasing part in the future ministry, if it is eliminated, Christianity will be that much the poorer.

The tradition of continence, virginity, and celibacy, despite its aberrations, is too long and persistent in the history of the Christian Church (and not by any means unknown in other religions) to deny the work of the Spirit in it. We may conclude that even if a married clergy is reestablished in the West, the spirit will continue to guide some souls to forsake marriage for a life of special relationship with him for the sake of the Kingdom. Either single or in community, lay or cleric, they would continue to live not proud of their calling or boasting of their continence, but as a humble spiritual leaven among the people of God.

Finally, although the return to earlier and simpler forms of the liturgy and ministry may bring an increase in fervor, we ought also to heed the early warnings against false prophets and teachers, against schisms and heresies, uniting all around the bishop, the center of unity and the guardian of tradition with the Roman church in the West as the true measure of the Apostolic tradition.

GENERAL BIBLIOGRAPHY

Audet, J., *Structures of the Christian Priesthood*, New York, Sheed & Ward, 1967.

Batiffol, P., *Primitive Catholicism*, New York, Longmans, Green & Co., 1911.

Baus, K., *From the Apostolic Community to Constantine*, New York, Herder & Herder, 1964.

Burkhart, B., "The Rise of the Christian Priesthood," *Journal of Religion*, 22 (1942), 187ff.

Chadwick, H., *The Early Church*, Baltimore, Penguin, 1967.

Colson, J., *L'évêque dans les communautés primitives*, Unam Sanctam 21, Paris, Cerf, 1951.

.... , *Les fonctions ecclésiales aux deux primiers siècles*, Paris, Desclee de Brouwer, 1956.

.... , *L'épiscopat catholique, collégialité, et primauté dans les trois primiers siècles de l'église*, Unam Sanctam 43, Paris, Cerf, 1963.

.... , *Ministre de Jésus Christ ou le sacerdoce de l'évangile*, Theologie Historique 4, Paris, Beauchesne, 1966.

Congar, Y., and B. DuPay, eds., *L'episcopat et l'église universelle*, Unam Sanctam 34, Paris, Cerf, 1962.

Danielou, J., and H. Marrou, *The First Six Hundred Years*, tr., V. Cronin, The Christian Centuries, vol. 1, New York, McGraw-Hill, 1964.

Davies, J., *The Early Christian Church*, New York, Holt, Rinehart & Winston, 1965.

Denzinger, H., and A. Schönmetzer, *Enchiridion Symbolorum*, New York, Herder & Herder, 1963.

D'Ercole, G., *Vescovi, Presbyteri e Laici alle Origine del Christianismo*, Rome, 1963.

Dix, G., *The Shape of the Liturgy*, Westminster, Dacre, 1949.

Eusebius, *The Ecclesiastical History*, two vols., Loeb Series, Cambridge Mass., Harvard University Press.

Gore, G., *The Church and the Ministry*, revised by C. Turner, London,

Longmans, 1919.

Gough, M., *The Early Christians,* New York, Praeger, 1961.

Harnack, A. von, *History of Dogma,* 7 vols., tr., N. Buchanan, New York, Russell & Russell, 1958.

.........................., *Die Mission und Ausbreitung des Christentums,* Leipzig, J. C. Hinrichs, 1924.

Jalland, T., *The Origin and Evolution of the Christian Church,* London, Hutchinson's University Library, 1948.

Jenkins, C., and K. MacKenzie, *Episcopacy, Ancient and Modern,* London, SPCK, 1930.

Jungmann, J., *The Place of Christ in Liturgical Prayer,* tr., A. Peeler, Staten Island, Alba House, 1965.

.........................., *The Early Liturgy,* tr., F. Brunner, University of Notre Dame Press, 1959.

.........................., *Public Worship,* tr., C. Howell, Collegeville, The Liturgical Press, 1957.

Kirk, K., ed., *The Apostolic Ministry,* London, Hodder & Stoughton, 1946.

Lampe, G., ed., *A Patristic Greek Lexikon,* Oxford, Clarendon, 1961.

Lebreton, J., and J. Zeiller, *History of the Primitive Church,* two vols., New York, Macmillan, 1949.

Lockton, W., *Divers Orders of Ministers,* London, Longmans, 1930.

Monson, T., *The Church's Ministry,* London, Hodder & Stoughton, 1948.

Moignt, J., "Caractère et ministère sacerdotale," *Recherches de Science Religieuse,* 56 (1968), pp. 563-589.

Niebuhr, H. R., and D. Williams, *The Ministry in Historical Perspective,* New York, Harper & Bros., Publishers, 1956.

Quasten, J., *Patrology,* three vols., Westminster, Md., Newman Press, 1950.

Rouet De Journel, M. J., *Enchiridion Patristicum,* Barcelona, Herder, 1959.

Sacrament of Holy Orders, The, Collegeville, Minn., The Liturgical Press, 1962.

Stevenson, J., ed., *A New Eusebius,* London, SPCK, 1968.

Streeter, B., *The Primitive Church with Special Reference to the Origins of the Christian Ministry*, London, Macmillan, 1929.

Swete, H., ed., *Essays on the Early History of the Church and the Ministry*, London, 1918.

SPECIAL BIBLIOGRAPHY

Chapter I: Jewish Presbyters.

Abrahams, I., *Studies in Pharisaism and the Gospels*, two vols., New York, KTAV Publishing House, 1961.

Baron, S., *A Social and Religious History of the Jews*, three vols., New York, Columbia University Press, 1937.

Ehrhardt, A., "Jewish and Christian Ordination," *Journal of Ecclesiastical History*, 5 (1954), pp. 125-138.

Finkelstein, L., *The Pharisees*, two vols., Philadelphia, The Jewish Publication Society, 1966.

Gavin, F., *The Jewish Antecedents of the Christian Sacraments*, London, SPCK, 1928.

Josephus, *Antiquities* and *Jewish War*, Loeb Series, Cambridge, Mass., Harvard University Press.

Lifshitz, B., "Fonctions et titres honorifiques dans les communautés juives, notes d'épigraphie palestinienne," *Rev. Bib.*, 67 (1960), pp. 58-64.

Mantel, H., *Studies in the History of the Sanhedrin*, Harvard Semitic Series XVII, Cambridge, Mass., Harvard University Press, 1961.

The Mishnah, tr., H. Danby, Oxford, 1964.

The Oxford Annotated Bible with Apocrypha, New York, Oxford University Press, 1965.

Schwank, B., "Qualis erat Forma Synagogarum Novi Testamenti," *Verb. Dom.*, 33 (1955), pp. 267-279.

The Talmud, London, Soncino Press, 1935.

Chapter II: *Christian Presbyters of the New Testament*.

Danielou, J., "La communauté de Qumran et l'organization de l'église ancienne," *Rev. Hist. Phil. Rel.*, 35 (1955), pp. 104-116.

Kittel, G., ed., *Theologisches Wörterbuch zum Neuen Testament*, especially articles on "diakonos," "episkopos," "presbyteros," Stuttgart, Kohlhammer, 1933; Grand Rapids, Eerdmans.

McKenzie, J., *Authority in the Church*, New York, Sheed & Ward, 1966.

Schweizer, E., *Church Order in the New Testament*, tr., F. Clarke, London, SCM, 1961.

Spicq, C., "L'origin évangélique des vertus épiscopales selon saint Paul," *Rev. Bib.*, Jan., 1946, pp. 36-46.

........................, *Les epîtres pastorales de saint Paul*, Etudes Bibliques, Paris, Le Coffre, 1947.

........................, *Spiritualità Sacerdotale in San Paolo*, Rome, Edizioni Paoline, 1952.

Strack, H., and P. Billerbeck, *Kommentar zum Neuen Testament aus Talmud und Midrash*, Munich, Beck, 1922-1928.

Chapter III: *Prophets and Presbyters of the Second Century*.

The Apostolic Fathers, R. Grant, ed., 6 vols., New York, Thomas Nelson & Sons, 1964-1968.

Bardy, G., *The Church at the End of the First Century*, London, Sands & Co. Ltd., 1938.

Barnard, L., "The Early Roman Church, Judaism and Jewish Christianity," *Ang. Theol. Rev.*, 49 (1967), pp. 371-384.

Blenkinsopp, J., "Presbyter to Priest: Ministry in the Early Church," *Worship*, 41 (Aug.-Sept. 1967), pp. 371-384.

Early Christian Fathers, tr., C. Richardson, Philadelphia, The Westminster Press, 1953, (LCC vol. 1).

Ehrhardt, A., *The Apostolic Succession in the First Two Centuries of
the Church,* London, 1953.

Filson, F., "The Christian Teacher in the First Century," *Jnl. of Bibl.
Lit.,* 60 (1941), pp. 317-328.

Guillet, J., "From Synagogue to Early Christian Community," *Life
Spir.,* 12 (1957), pp. 22-29; 64-73.

Goppelt, L., *Christentum und Judentum im 1 und 2 Jarhundert, ein
Aufriss der Urgeschicte der Kirche,* Gutersloh, Bertelsmann, 1954.

Parkes, J., *The Conflict of the Church and Synagogue,* Cleveland, World,
1961.

Strecker, G., "Christentum und Judentum in den ersten beiden Jahrhund-
erten," *Evang. Theol.,* 16 (1956), pp. 458-477.

Chapter IV: Presbyters Become Priests: Third Century Church Order.

The Ante-Nicene Fathers, A. Roberts and J. Donaldson, eds., 10 vols.,
New York, Charles Scribner's Sons, 1926.

The Apostolic Tradition of Hippolytus, tr., intro., notes, B. Easton,
Cambridge University Press, 1934.

Camphausen, H. von, *The Fathers of the Greek Church,* tr., S. Godman,
New York, Pantheon, 1955.

........................, *Men Who Shaped the Western Church,* New York,
Harper & Row, Publishers, 1965.

Didascalia Apostolorum, tr., intro., notes, R. Connolly, Oxford, Clarendon
Press, 1929.

Hardy, E., *Christian Egypt: Church and People,* New York, Oxford
University Press, 1952.

Oulton, J., and H. Chadwick, *Alexandrian Christianity,* (LCC vol. 2),
Philadelphia, The Westminster Press.

Telfer, W., "Episcopal Succession in Egypt," *Jnl. of Eccl. Hist.*, 3 1952), pp. 1-13.

Walker, G., *The Churchmanship of St. Cyprian*, Richmond, Va., John Knox Press, 1969.

Chapter V: *The Sacred and the Secular: Fourth Century Sacerdotalism.*

Gryson, R., *Le prête selon saint Ambrose*, Louvain, edition orientaliste, 1968.

Hefele, C., *A History of the Church Councils*, 6 vols., Edinburgh, T. & T. Clark, 1872.

John Chrysostom, *On the Priesthood*, tr., P. Boyle, Westminster, Md., Newman Press, 1955.

Pellegrino, M., *The True Priest: the Priesthood as Preached and Practiced by Saint Augustine*, tr., A. Gibson, New York, Philosophical Library, 1968.

Schillebeeckx, E., *Celibacy*, tr., C. Jarrett, New York, Sheed & Ward, 1968.

Select Letters of St. Jerome, tr., F. Wright, New York, G. P. Putnam's Sons, 1933, (Loeb Classical Library).

A Select Library of the Nicene and Post-Nicene Fathers, ed., P. Schaff, New York, Charles Scribner's Sons, 1908-1914.

Socrates, *The Ecclesiastical History*, London, Geo. Bell & Sons, 1874.

Sozomen, *The Ecclesiastical History*, also the *Ecclesiastical History* of Philostorgius, London, Henry G. Bohn, 1855.

Stevenson, J., *Creeds, Councils, and Controversies*, New York, Seabury Press, 1966.

The Theodosian Code and Novels and the Sirmondian Constitutions, tr., C. Pharr, Princeton University Press, 1952.

INDEX OF SUBJECTS

INDEX OF PERSONS